THE BOOK OF CHAI

MIRA MANEK

THE BOOK OF CHAI

HISTORY, STORIES AND MORE THAN 60 RECIPES

First published in 2024 by Headline Home
an imprint of Headline Publishing Group

1

Cataloguing in Publication Data is available from the British Library.

Hardback ISBN 978 1 0354 0223 6
eISBN 978 1 0354 0224 3

Map artwork by Owen Delaney

Designed and set by EM&EN
Printed and bound in Great Britain by Clays Ltd, Elcograf S.p.A.

Headline's policy is to use papers that are natural, renewable and recyclable
products and made from wood grown in well-managed forests and other
controlled sources. The logging and manufacturing processes are expected
to conform to the environmental regulations of the country of origin.

HEADLINE PUBLISHING GROUP
An Hachette UK Company
Carmelite House
50 Victoria Embankment
London EC4Y 0DZ

www.headline.co.uk
www.hachette.co.uk

For my grandparents

And for the labourers and their families
who worked on the tea plantations many years ago,
living in unthinkable conditions and treated like slaves,
many of whom lost their lives.

Contents

Himalayas

KASHMIR

PAKISTAN

CHINA

Kangra

▲ Mount Kailas

Kurukshetra

Dehradun
Rishikesh
Haridwar

HARYANA

Delhi

Ganges

NEPAL

SIKKIM BHUTAN

Darjeeling
Dooars

ASSAM

Varanasi

BIHAR

BANGLADESH

GUJARAT

Ahmedabad

● Bhopal

WEST
BENGAL

Junagadh

INDIA

Kolkata

MAHARASHTRA

● Mumbai

BAY

OF

● Chennai

BENGAL

WESTERN
GHATS

Nilgiris
Ootacamund

N

India through chai

Preface

Life changes. The things you know as truths change. Relationships change. Letting go of the old and accepting the new is a wonderful thing once you realise that's all you can do. Washing in and away like a wave, becoming still like the water in the middle of the ocean and eventually meeting the horizon. After shedding, grieving, receiving, after so many realisations.

When I see my grandmother now, almost three years after the death of my grandfather, that's where she is. The broken part of her, which I witnessed for so long after his death, remembering his habits, his daily routine, his love for her, that very fragmented part slowly healed. Suddenly, the way summer comes after winter and changes the entire landscape, my grandmother started speaking about the *Bhagavad Gita*, her daily reading and learnings, about Krishna, about the stories in this universal text, and she started laughing again when she relayed these stories, bringing them to life.

Like sitting in the temple, lighting a diya candle and praying, like boiling her morning cup of chai with spices and sipping it slowly with breakfast, like her daily stretches, it is these rituals that carry us through, small rituals of happiness, dependable and purposeful, that we inject into life

It is in these last few years, after writing my second book *Prajñā: Ayurvedic Rituals for Happiness*, that I have started to realise the true value of my daily rituals, that happiness is a constant work in progress, that what once lifted me will lift me again, because the challenges life throws at us won't stop, but our ability to overcome them changes. And while the rituals might change from time to time, commitment to them and consistency in practice is what matters.

So – keep making time for those small things that, together, bring big joy, moments that feel like a sigh, that ground you, like making your chai with spices, grating ginger or crushing cardamom pods, savouring each sip as you read or journal or simply sit. Pick a new ritual each month and become consistent with it: yoga, strength training, massaging your face with oil, seeing your friends more or even reading a book – everyone's starting point is different. Lastly, do something that challenges you, and relax into discomfort, because that's where you'll grow. The waves will keep coming, relationships will keep changing, things will get washed way, even people, but something new will also flow in. Your rituals will help you find that abundance, let go with grace and not just tread the water, but ride the waves with more calm.

I set out to write this dedication to my grandfather, but what came out was an ode to my grandmother, whom I still see almost daily. Besides, it was coffee, boiled in a pan, that was his daily ritual, twice a day, measured and consistent, as with everything he did. I always wondered why he never drank chai!

Introduction

'Come oh come ye tea-thirsty restless ones – the kettle boils, bubbles and sings, musically.'

– Rabindranath Tagore

In India, masala chai – a strong, sweet and milky tea brewed with spices, with its unique and exhilarating aroma – is woven into the very fabric of life. In most Indian homes, it's the ritual that starts the day and the first thing offered to guests, the cornerstone of Indian hospitality. The scent of the simmering spices in the early morning lifts the spirits before even a drop is drunk; during the day it serves as a punctuation mark, a time to stop and reawaken; for some, it is a ritual to end the day with calmness, like a big sigh; and neighbourhood gossips and political discussions happen over a cup of chai. You'll find it on streets and in hotels; you'll be served chai while you're shopping for saris; at railway stations, chai is a staple stop on a road journey; and it is the drink that keeps the babas, saints and pilgrims awake at religious festivals.

Whether at the break of dawn, or mid-morning, noon, evening or even late at night, chai is always on the boil both in the homes and on the streets of India. It is the social lubricant for all occasions, ceremonies and transactions; and the cult term 'chai pe charcha', meaning 'gossip over chai', is a testament to the unparalleled popularity of chai in India. Chai wakes India up and keeps her people going. In fact, the process of brewing and boiling tea feels so steeped in tradition and recent history that it is arguably on par with curry as an international symbol of Indian cuisine. In some ways drinking chai is synonymous with being Indian.

So how did this happen? With over three and a half million hectares of the earth's surface covered by tea plantations, it is no wonder that tea is the most popular beverage in the world, after water, and India consumes more tea than any other country globally – in 2022, the amount of tea consumed in India was approximately 1.2 billion kilograms. As we'll see in Chapter 2, though, the history of tea in India is relatively recent. So how did India become the second-largest tea producer in the world (after China) with around a $10 billion market?

Reading about the somewhat mysterious history of chai in my research for this book was both fascinating and surprising. Tracing the exact dates of when tea leaves first arrived in India, to when tea was first brewed, when and why spices were added, and then of course milk, and when Indians all over the country started drinking chai as their daily drink, is almost impossible. It is just as difficult to trace the origins of tea before it arrived in India, although that tea was first cultivated in China is an unquestioned historical fact. The history of drinking different concoctions of spices in hot water, known as 'kadha', is far older in India, and is expounded in the ancient Ayurveda texts. How tea and spices were then married to create masala chai is in fact a slight mystery, but what is clear is that the spices add a plethora of medicinal benefits to the tea. I hope you enjoy this voyage of discovery along with me.

My love for chai

My own love affair with chai started in childhood. At breakfast time, my siblings and I would be served a cup of ukaro (chai masala spice mix with milk and sugar, but no tea) with buttered toast most mornings or, as a treat on the weekends, we might drink it accompanied by fresh puri (fluffy, yellow, deep-fried breads). My mum, my two aunts and my grandmother would all be bustling about the small white kitchen of our home, cooking and doing domestic chores as we children drank our chai, and, if it was a puri morning, a steel basin of these delicious, crisp breads would be sitting temptingly in the middle of the table.

Ukaro, lacking in tea leaves and therefore caffeine, is perfect for children. In Gujarati, the word 'ukaro', or 'ukar', means 'to boil', and it is the boiling of the milk with the spices that allows the powdered spices to fully assimilate. I can still call to mind the slight tinge of brown in the white milk, with the occasional clump of bubbles on the top from pouring. A particularly handy trick was to tip a little of this hot and comforting drink from our porcelain cup into the small white saucer to cool it down, all so that we could drink it – or rather slurp it – more quickly. Better yet, I'd dunk my toast or puri in the ukaro too, so as to enjoy that wonderful gooey texture into the bargain.

Later on, travelling in India as a teenager, my memory conjures up visions of chaiwalas (tea vendors) pouring chai from high above into glass cups, creating froth and steam, street-side performances that stayed with me, as did the syrupy sweetness of the chai I drank. Though possibly my most vivid memory from that time is actually of coffee-pouring in Thiruvananthapuram, South India, on a trip with my dad, where we watched a particularly skilful street vendor pour boiling-hot milky coffee from one glass cup high up in the air to another very low down, moving the glasses in a balancing act to ensure no milk was spilled, almost like a juggling act. We'll cover the coffee traditions of India later on in this book (see page 125), alongside those of chai.

In my early twenties, the chai theme continued, when I titled my unpublished novel inspired by my grandmother's childhood stories *Chai by the Lake*. As a teenager, visiting my grandmother's home village in Gujarat with my brother brought to life the elaborate tales she used to tell me, growing up with her own nani (maternal grandmother), fetching water from the lake, working in the field. And so the vision of the two of us sitting around the eponymous lake drinking our milky brews was a rich creative prompt, like the famous Proustian madeleine. She still tells me stories, always with vivid detail, some of which I've written about in this book.

During my university days chai was a constant: boiling tea leaves in milk and water (always plenty of milk for me), serving the hot drink in a mug rather than a cup, and making the mix extra spicy, which meant more ginger. My favourite and easiest accompaniment to chai at that time tended to be khakhra, a thin and crisp toasted roti, so moreish I could probably still eat quite a few of these in one go today. Recalling a rather lonely year at university, when I was yo-yo dieting, one image returns to me clearly: boiling a large mug of chai after my morning workout, with skimmed milk, using the small jar of chai masala mix my mum had packed for me. I would sit at my desk and the chai would provide a few moments of calm – some much-needed headspace and a moment to just be. Later on, as I travelled and lived abroad in Dubai and Uganda and worked as a food and travel writer, chai was always my happy place, the one steady thing that would fill me, fuel me, comfort me; a ritual of calmness and being in the moment.

And chai is that – it is a moment to stop, to inhale, to feel awakened by the heady concoction of tea leaves and spices, a moment to look out of the window and observe, to sit and let thoughts waft into thin air like the steam from the chai, a moment to breathe and sigh, to feel the heat of the spices absorb into the body, to feel the senses awaken from the tea, and for the sweetness to send a rush of energy to the brain. And this ephemeral sensory experience happens whether or not you're conscious of it, whether you're having chai alone or as the accompaniment to your gossip or catch-up, known as 'chai pe charcha' in India. When I think of chai pe charcha, I remember post-mortems of parties, and nights out with my closest friends and family – sitting with my sister Meenal, discussing family events, something momentous or even everyday that had recently happened; breathing in the air on the sea-facing balcony of my friend Sunaina's home in Bandra, Mumbai, listening to the waves in the dark of the night as we drank cinnamon tea and spoke about the night we'd just had, or first thing the next morning, still in our pyjamas, sipping a restorative chai while watching the water roll inland and wash over the rocks; or more recently a morning in the lush rainforest of Ubud, Bali, where my friend Simran made us her morning ritual cup of Darjeeling tea, slightly smoky and with no milk or masala, and we sat and chatted about the previous night's gallery opening party, laughing about the amount we danced, commiserating over our lack of sleep and exploring our love of books, life in India, politics and more.

When I moved back to London after living in Dubai and Uganda, and my marriage came to an end, I started a career in food and wellness almost by accident. I was working as a cookery writer, and I happened to take some home-made spiced energy balls that I'd made for a magazine to a couple of cafés I loved. The owners tried the balls, and soon afterwards started selling them in their cafés and delis. At a similar time I created a chai spice mix (without sugar), wanting to offer it to customers the way I had always had it with my family at home. One of my clients tried the potent mix and asked if I could create a ready-to-use version of it including sugar. That, in a nutshell, is how my business, Chai by Mira, came about. I started selling the spice mix direct to businesses, and a few years later I launched my café, also called Chai by Mira, in Triyoga Soho, a central London yoga studio. As the name suggests, the café was centred around chai offerings, with everything from Chai Latte to Rose Chai – recipes you'll find in this book – as well as wholesome Ayurvedic food. Regulars soon had their favourite blends and would come to meet friends, sip chai after a yoga class or just sit and read – we had two shelves of beautiful books to browse through. Everything in my café, from the ragas playing in the background (you can find the playlists in my book, *Prajñā*), was designed in such a way that it would inspire people to sit down for some peace and quiet, to have that ritual moment with a cup of chai, away from the bustle of the city.

Alongside everything else, we sold small packets of the chai spice blend in the café. During the first summer of the Covid pandemic and lockdowns, I started receiving queries about where to buy the spice mix. People were missing their chai! In response, I set up the Chai by Mira brand online, and have gone on to create many blends of different flavours. Eventually the online business expanded to such an extent that I decided not to reopen the café.

About this book

The idea for *The Book of Chai* came about a year after I launched my online business. To my delight, writing this book has been an enriching, eye-opening and therapeutic experience, rather like chai itself. Even though I've always loved drinking chai, I discovered so much more about the fascinating global history of tea and spices through my research.

I've also delved deep into my treasure chest of precious travel memories. There are stories of India and of my own journeys woven through with cups of chai in this book, from holy festivals in faraway places to the Mumbai monsoons, and even during a pause from white-water rafting in Rishikesh. For me, chai is also about family, so there are stories of my grandmother, whom we call Bhabhi, and her chai memories interlaced into stories of growing up in a village in Gujarat, her year of yatra (pilgrimage) when she returned to India as a mother of three, and of the summers I spent with my mother at her parents' home in Loughborough, England.

I hope this paints in your mind a vision of the old and new India and the diaspora, with interlinked aspects of history, elements of culture and an essence of spirituality. I hope it transports you to the ethereal ghats of Varanasi, brings to life the naga bavas with matted hair smoking ganja at the festival of Mahashivratri, and makes you feel like you're waking up after an overnight train journey from Bihar sipping chai with strangers. I hope it stirs within you a desire to explore and journey through this rich and colourful country, savouring cups of chai and eating authentic street and dhaba food, and reminds you of sharing your favourite meals and drinks with your loved ones. I hope these stories paint a picture so vivid you can visualise yourself in those moments, a cup of chai in your hand – and that they inspire you not only to make some of the food and drink from this book, but to travel and create your own stories and memories.

Finally, there's a plethora of recipes, from various tea-based chais boiled with spices and herbs to healthy Ayurvedic concoctions, and lassis and milks with different spices. I've offered some savoury accompaniments to go with your chai, including chaats (snacks) and even chilli cheese toasties. I've also created breakfast and dessert recipes using chai spices, from Apple Crumble Baked Oats to Carrot Cake Masala Chai Cupcakes.

Each time you pick up this book, I suggest you make yourself a cup of chai – perhaps a Golden Chai if it's evening, a Ginger Chai if it's morning, or an Ayurvedic spice blend in hot water if you want a post-meal digestif. Take a deep breath and smell the aroma: the spices, the tea leaves, the sweetness. Stop, take a few more deep breaths, and smile; when you take your first sip, close your eyes, allow yourself to sigh, and arrive into the present moment. Feel the smile; settle into the smile; and let the smile settle into you.

What is Chai?

'Just forget all about enlightenment. Enjoy simple things with total intensity. Just a cup of tea can be a deep meditation. If you can enjoy it, the aroma of it, slowly sipping it, the taste of it . . . who cares about God?'

– Osho

Chai is a global phenomenon. For many of us in the West, when we think of chai we picture spiced, milky Indian tea, variously known as chai, chai latte, chai tea latte, chai tea and masala chai. But is there a difference? Why so many names? Let's delve in a bit.

The different names

When I was growing up, my mum, grandmother and aunts made their daily chai by boiling tea leaves with milk, grated ginger and their own home-made chai spice powder blend. This is what I took chai to mean: tea boiled with spices, the key differentiating factor from 'normal' tea being the spices. Chai, however, simply means tea – not tea with milk, not tea with milk and spices, just tea! What I thought of as chai, the milky, boiled, spiced, sweet and strong version, is actually masala chai. Nowadays, chai has become much more common, and it has as many definitions as there are retailers. Supermarkets sell ready-made chai blends to add to milk or water, and you'll usually now find teabags labelled 'chai', too. In addition, coffee houses like Starbucks offer hot spiced drinks, usually called chai lattes. Although these beverages have been eagerly embraced as part of metropolitan café culture, in my opinion attempts to adapt chai to western tastes generally lose something in translation, often being flavoured with vanilla- or cinnamon-infused syrups and packed with sugar, but not including enough spice for my taste.

The etymology of the word 'chai' is also fascinating! In Hindi, the language spoken throughout much of India, 'chai' is the word for 'tea leaves', as well as for the drink itself. In both Mandarin and Cantonese, both the beverage and the leaf are called 'chai-i' or 'chai-e', although in some parts of China and in certain dialects, tea is called 'te'. Tea of any kind is also called chai in Russian.

Chai in India

Hot, strong, spicy, milky, sweet and syrupy, chai in India is the first ritual of the day, it is the essential lubricant of all social occasions from weddings to meetings, it is the energy fuel for rickshaw-wallahs, labourers and business owners – indeed, everything happens over a cup of chai. It is difficult to imagine an India without chai. There are so many different ways of making it, and in India today they vary by region, by family or even between different members of the same family. Some people simply boil milk and tea with grated ginger, some use crushed cardamom, others add lemongrass, fresh mint leaves, saffron and fennel. Most Indian families and chaiwalas (tea vendors) have their own special blend of ground spices (masala) that they use to make their chai, which will be a source of pride and often a well-kept secret. And there are just as many ways of drinking chai too, from serving it in a clay 'kulhad' cup to sipping it from a saucer (almost always audibly slurped). There are even regional variations in temperature, with some people preferring their chai 'garam', meaning piping hot. And whatever type of chai is served, it is usually accompanied by a delicious snack. These can be savoury and even spicy to balance out the sweetness of the chai – from samosa, dhokla (savoury sponge cake) and thepla (flatbreads) to puff pastry biscuits and fried cutlets – or you may find your chai served with some sweet biscuits, such as the famous Parle-G (see page 222).

The culture of tea-drinking in roadside restaurants known as dhabas brings people from all walks of life together. It's more prevalant in North India, whereas in South India you'll find tiffin rooms, rather like canteens, which open early for breakfast, serving idlis (savoury rice and lentil cakes), dosas (savoury crispy pancakes), vadas (fritters) and upma (savoury porridge), typical South Indian cuisine, with the mandatory aromatic South Indian filter coffee. There is a tea culture here too, but chai is called chaya, and often brewed just with milk and sugar, and accompanied by snacks native to the region, like pazhampori (banana fritters), parippu vada (lentil fritters) and murukku (crispy snacks made with rice and lentil flour). Some South Indians make chai with lemongrass or bay leaves, and I explore some recipes for these on pages 88 and 91.

In Rajasthan, in northern India, the chai is more 'kadak' or strong, and is mainly drunk from traditional kulhad (cups made of clay), with ample sugar to replenish drinkers exhausted by the intense desert heat. However, there is also another thick and milky tea called Nagori chai, which comes from remote parts of Rajasthan. The Nagori community originates from the central Rajasthani region of Nagaur, and its members are mostly Muslim. Interestingly, they were marble tile manufacturers for almost seven decades, until some forty years ago, when much of the community took up dairy farming.

You'll find Nagori chai shops in the southern city of Mumbai and other cities, serving a tea that uses fresh, unpasteurised cow's milk sourced directly from the farmers, making it milkier and sweeter than other types of Indian tea. In Nagori tea shops, you will also find milk being boiled on one side in a big vessel, thick and creamy, which some like to drink on its own, but which is used for making the tea. Most Nagori chai shops will often also sell other milk-based products, such as paneer (cheese), dahi (curd) and ghee (clarified butter).

Travel to the other side of India and Kolkata (formerly Calcutta) in the East Indian state of West Bengal, and you'll find it the chai capital of India, because it is the geographical gateway to the tea gardens. You'll find chai everywhere, with multiple trolleys on one street in the main city areas. The traditional earthen kulhad are known in Kolkata as 'bhar'. These cups are made of clay called gangamati, meaning 'clay of the

Ganga', which is dug from the banks of Ganges, India's most sacred river. Kulhads are used all over India, though cheaper plastic and paper cups have replaced them in many regions, but they are environmentally friendly and can be thrown on the ground after use. In Kolkata, the tradition has been preserved.

The tea itself is also less milky in Kolkata, as the tea leaves are considered more important there. You will also find lemon chai, known as lebu chai, in Kolkata and the eastern parts of India, which is a spiced and salted lemon tea brewed with delicate tea leaves, often served up with momos, popular savoury dumplings. In his book *The Monk as Man: The Unknown Life of Swami Vivekanand*, Mani Sankar Mukherji writes, 'Bengalis have tea in their blood and nobody can do anything about it. Bengalis will never forget that coffee smells like burnt shal leaf, while Darjeeling tea tastes like champagne.' Rabindranath Tagore (1861–1941), a prolific nationalist and world-renowned writer, poet and philosopher from Kolkata, as well as the first Indian to receive the Nobel Prize for Literature, was the grandson of Dwarkanath Tagore, who, as we'll see on page 29, was a key player in the origins of the tea business in India alongside the British, as one of the nine founding directors of the Bengal Tea Association.

Among the earliest formal venues for tea or chai were the 'tea cabins' of Kolkata which started springing up in the 1920s in neighbourhoods near universities, offering inexpensive tea and snacks. Tea cabins were basic cafés with marble-top tables and wooden chairs, serving drinks alongside toast, omelettes and cutlets. They brewed tea by combining a full-leaf tea with a little milk and sugar just before serving. These spots became hubs for news, political gossip and cultural discussions, backdrops for intellectual movements, some of them even publishing their own literary or political journals; and, decades later, they became important meeting places for those planning India's independence.

Irani cafés in Mumbai, on the opposite coast, came about at a similar time and also became social hubs. Established in the nineteenth century by Zoroastrian immigrants, who were fleeing religious persecution in what was then Persia (now Iran), like other purveyors of tea these cafés became meeting places for people from all castes, religion and classes, where writers found solace, construction labourers and sex workers could come and pay less than a rupee for chai, and eventually here too people met to hatch plans for India's independence. These were the foundation of Mumbai's restaurant and nightlife culture, an integral part of the city's sense of self and history. There are some left, but from the 350 Irani cafés that existed in 1950, just after independence, there are now fewer than a hundred left. Along with hot Irani chai (see page 100), you might also get bun maska (sweet bread rolls), egg akuri (spiced scrambled egg), mawa cakes (rich, buttery, eggless cakes) baked in tinfoil containers, and kheema pao (minced meat with bread). I write more about these cafés on page 100.

The Zoroastrian community of India also includes the Parsis, who trace their roots to a community who arrived from Iran in the tenth century. Parsis have their chai in a way that's entirely different to everyone else. Steeping tea leaves, lemongrass and mint leaves in hot water, they then cover the kettle with a tea cosy to keep it hot as the tea and leaves brew, and add hot milk and sugar separately when the tea is poured. In the mornings, the Parsi tradition is to serve chai with brun bread, which has a crackling crust and is soft inside, slathered with butter and totally 'dunkable'. In the afternoon, chai is served with Batasa cookies – small round biscuits studded with carom (caraway) seeds, whose history dates back to the Dutch occupation of

India in the 1700s. A man named Faramji Dotivala in the port city of Surat took control of a flourishing bakery and created Batasa biscuits from left-over dried breads. Over two centuries and six generations later, the bakery still exists.

In Bhopal, Central India, chai is made with salt, and is known as namak wali chai, which translates as 'tea with salt', and is claimed to have health benefits, such as soothing the throat. There are numerous tea shops here that prepare salted chai, starting the boiling process at 4 a.m., cooking the milk until it becomes creamy, and making the tea strong and mildly salted. Bhopal used to have a poetry culture and youngsters would sit on patiyas (wooden benches), write and share soulful shayaris (poetry), while drinking this salted chai, so this delicacy still lives on today.

In Kashmir, the base is made with green tea and baking soda, which turns the chai pink, while the Parsis created the distinctively creamy Irani Chai (see page 100). In Assam and in most of north eastern India, locals drink lal cha, black tea, without any milk but with ample sugar. The colour of the tea is reddish-brown, hence 'Lal' cha, 'lal' meaning red. In Sikkim, Ladakh and other parts of Tibet, where the winters can be freezing and harsh, they have a butter chai, made with ghee or yak butter and salt to keep them warm. In addition to the warmth it provides, the addition of salt to this tea helps Tibetans stay hydrated in the cold Himalayan Mountains as the human body loses water roughly twice as fast as it would at sea level at high altitudes above 10,000 feet, making the risk of dehydration high. In *The Story of Tea*, authors Mary Lou and Robert Heiss describe how a Chinese princess was married to the king of Tibet, opening up tea and other trade between the two countries.

It is worth noting that tea will vary from region to region not only due to the milk content, but also the type of water used. Making tea with hard or more alkaline water will produce a different flavour to tea made with acidic water.

Chaiwalas

So that's a whistle-stop tour through the styles of tea in different regions. But if you're not in a tiffin room, dhaba or café, how do you purchase your chai? In India, a 'wallah' is someone who makes or sells a certain good, and thus a chai-wallah or chaiwala is someone who makes and sells chai. You'll find these vendors all over India, from the streets of Mumbai to the deserts of Rajasthan, at train stations, at religious melas (festivals), outside temples, gurudwaras and masjids, by the ghats of the Ganges in Rishikesh and Varanasi – everywhere!

What I love most about having chai on the street is watching the chaiwala make the drink – it really is street theatre. The way he adds the ingredients so quickly your eyes can't keep up, noticing which spices he uses – does he grate ginger, add a powdered spice mix, or even pound cinnamon sticks, cardamom pods, cloves and black peppercorns in a mortar, or immerse long lemongrass stalks into the chai? Then, watching the brew boil on a large flame, so loud it competes with the cacophony of cars and lorries honking, you might start feeling the heat on your face in the scorching India weather and have to move away a little. As he rhythmically stirs the chai, its colour will swiftly change from a milky brown to a much deeper brown (again this will vary from chaiwala to chaiwala and region to region). He may add more tea leaves if it isn't as kadak as he likes; when the dancing bubbles start rising to the top of the pan, he may use a sandasi (kitchen pincer) to lift the pan and swirl it around before putting it back on the flame, or if it's too big to lift, reduce the heat slightly and keep swirling and lifting the chai brew with a long ladle, so adeptly that none of it spills as he lifts the ladle again and again – an orchestra with the chaiwala as conductor. Finally, once the chai is fully boiled – or rather, browned – he will have his own way of pouring the chai into a pot, a flask, a smaller pan or even directly into small cups. Often, chaiwalas will pour the chai into a chaidaan, an aluminium tea kettle that comes in different sizes, from which they then pour it into cups.

'*Garam chai!*' is the most common call of the chaiwala, or even '*Garam-aa-garam chai!*', which means 'hottest of the hot teas', something you will hear bellowed on railway platforms and bus stands all over India as the chaiwala runs up and down the platform carrying chai in a large flask in one hand and a stack of cups in the other, trying to jolt travellers awake from their naps as the train comes to a halt, passing cups of chai through the windows and doors in exchange for coins and small notes. You'll be able to put your finger on the pulse of a city and feel the rhythm of daily life by stopping at a local chai stand and having a chai.

So . . . is there an authentic way of making chai?

Having made chai in so many different ways and with all types of milks and having tried a whole range of chais from the varieities of chaiwala chais to the modern café chai lattes, I can tell you that there certainly isn't a best way – or even such a thing as a 'proper' chai. The strength of the tea or the strength of the spices, the texture of the chai, the milkiness or richness of the consistency, the sweetness – it's all a matter of preference, dictated for many by how they grew up drinking chai and therefore what they deem as 'proper', and for others by their palate, how much spice they like and whether they love tea. For me, the spices matter the most. I prefer a spicier chai, especially because each spice has such a wealth of health benefits (which we'll cover in Chai Ingredients, page 50) and I love all things that help my body and make me feel warmer, calmer and better. When I have chai, it's like a big, deep sigh.

Today, chai is the answer to every problem and every ailment: it helps to oil the wheels of Indian society, and everything from neighbourly gossip and business deals to political discussions and religious rituals happens over a cup of chai. Wherever you are in the world, a refreshing drink is so often the accompaniment when we come together with family, with friends, with passers-by, for conversation and a moment to pause. India is the same, only it's chai – and it's literally everywhere you go and at all times of day.

A Brief History of Tea

'If you are cold, tea will warm you; if you are too heated, it will cool you; if you are depressed, it will cheer you; if you are excited, it will calm you.'

– William E. Gladstone (1809–98)

Despite its status as one of the most ubiquitous drinks consumed by Indians, chai as we know it today was virtually non-existent in India before the 1900s. So, if Indians only started drinking tea around 120 years ago, and as we'll see, added spices and milk to the brew even later, how did this cherished habit become such an integral feature of the modern-day cultural identity of Indians, both in India and all over the world? And how did India become one of the world's top-five tea-exporting countries?

The rise of chai as India's national drink is a fascinating story and linked closely with India's identity. It is steeped in India's colonial past, in the Empire, and fuelled by the British obsession with tea, which started as an upper-class luxury but slowly trickled down to the middle and working classes. As we'll discover, the switch to widespread recreational tea-drinking in India came about under the rule of the British. But let's begin at the – quite mysterious – beginning.

Ancient myths and theories

We know that the Chinese had been drinking tea for over 2,000 years before it became sought after worldwide. There are many myths surrounding the discovery of the tea plant, but the most popular focus on the Chinese emperor Shennong, said to have ruled around 2700 BCE. He was venerated as the Father of Chinese medicine and, like all ancient Chinese emperors, considered divine. Legend has it that Shennong was drinking boiling water one day when leaves from a nearby tree blew into his pot, and the scent of the resulting brew intrigued him. When he drank it, he was amazed by its wonderful taste and restorative properties. And that is how 'cha' came to be, according to Chinese lore.

In Japanese culture it's said that tea was first discovered by Bodhidharma, the monk who founded the spiritual tradition in China that later spread to Japan and became Zen Buddhism. In one version of the story, during the fifth year of a seven-year sleepless meditation, Bodhidharma started to feel sleepy. Noticing a nearby bush, he plucked a few leaves and chewed them, and found his sleepiness disappeared. That bush was a wild tea plant. In another version, Bodhidharma is said to have removed his own eyelids to remain awake during meditation, and a tea plant began to grow where his eyelids landed. Teaism (tea-making and tea-drinking) took on deep religious significance in the fifteenth century, with the tea-room as the most important building, set apart from the house in a garden, where tea ceremonies were held.

Tea is now so inherently a part of cultural life in Japan that is difficult for the Japanese to conceive of a time with no tea in the temple gardens in Japan.

Indian theories date the discovery of tea back to the epic Hindu text the *Ramayana*, the events of which are said to have happened some 7,000 years ago. In one episode, Lakshman, younger brother of Lord Rama, is attacked and injured. The monkey god Hanuman seeks out a special mountain plant called Sanjeevani booti and flies back with it in one hand to save Lord Lakshman's life. It has been suggested that this shrub seems akin to the tea plant *Camellia sinensis*.

Another suggestion, made by Frederick R. Dannaway in the essay 'Tea as Soma' is that the Soma referred to many times in Indian sacred texts the *Rigveda* and *Bhagavad Gita*, a medicinal herb and divine elixir invoking a visionary state, was in fact tea. The word 'soma' first appeared around 3,500 years ago, praising the psychedelically induced states of the drink, although other writers have suggested that the word could refer to psychedelic mushrooms or even cannabis.

Early history

Whatever its mythical origins, historical records indicate that tea has been grown in India since at least 750 BCE, in the native tea plantations of the Assam jungles, although it was used medicinally and as a cooking ingredient rather than as a beverage. A tenth-century Sanskrit medical text from Assam called *Nidana* (*The Science of Diagnosis*), mentions leaves called 'shamapatra' from which a drink called 'shamapani' was made, which is thought to be the first mention of tea in India. The earliest tea-drinkers – the Singhpo and Khamti tribes of Assam – used tea as medicine, believing that a cup of brewed tea after every meal aids digestion. Hundreds of years later, the Dutch explorer Jan Huyghen von Linschoten, who visited Assam in

1538, noted that tribal people would prepare tea leaves with garlic and oil as a vegetable dish. Another few hundred years passed before records show the Singhpo chief Bisa Gaum met with Scottish merchant Robert Bruce in 1823 to explore the potential of tea. However, the Assam tea plant was so different to the Chinese plant that it took several years for the British to recognise it as tea. We'll explore more of this history on pages 27 to 33. According to contemporary historian Lu Yu, whose book on tea, *Ch'a Ching (The Classic of Tea)*, appeared around 780 CE, the use of tea had become so extensive in China by the eighth century that it was taxed. A huge trade in 'bricks of tea' grew up along the Silk Road, a network of important trading and caravan routes that wove across the mountains and deserts, linking China with the Far East, Central Asia, India, the Middle East and the Mediterranean. Over time, tea houses began to appear across large cities along the routes, making tea more accessible outside of elite society. According to historians Alan and Iris McFarlane, by about the twelfth century, these 'tea bricks' were so ubiquitous that they became the preferred currency in many parts of Central Asia. During the Ming dynasty (1368–1644 CE) tea-wares became a major art form, and these ceramics were exported as luxury trade items along the Silk Road.

Tea spread slowly from Asia to Europe, and arrived in Venice around 1560 CE. It was the Portuguese and Dutch traders who first imported tea further into Europe with regular shipments. By the end of the eighteenth century, tea-drinking was established more widely across the world.

British love of tea

In 1992's *The Book of Tea*, British writer Anthony Burgess baptised tea as 'a fact of British life, like breathing'. There is a popular fable, often repeated in modern writings on tea, that the British romance with the beverage began when the Portuguese princess Catherine of Braganza married Charles II in 1662. According to the story, she introduced tea-drinking to England by bringing the leaves with her as part of her dowry, along with the Indian city of Bombay. However, history tells us that tea was already arriving in England from 1645 from Holland, where Dutch ships brought small shipments of tea, nine years after they had started to send these to Paris. By the 1650s the shipments of Dutch tea to England had become regular and substantial enough for the London entrepreneur Thomas Garway to commence the public sale of tea at the Sultaness Head, a coffee-house near the Royal Exchange in London, in 1657.

Samuel Pepys's diary entry on 'tcha' (tea) of 25 September 1660 is one of the first major references to tea in England. Pepys recorded that the 'excellent and by all Physicians approved, China drink' was sold in England from 1635 for prices as high as £6–£10 per pound – equivalent to the annual rent the East India Company paid the British Crown for the whole of Bombay (£1,000–£1,700 in today's prices). So, we can assume tea had been known in England before the Dutch shipments, but probably not widely, because it was very expensive.

Pepys was not the first famous English tea-drinker, but for him 'tea represented a major shift in European material, medical, commercial, and culinary cultures'. As Pepys wrote, tea was 'Physician approved', and we know that tea at the time was being consumed as a medicine, supposedly invigorating the body and

The East India Company

The British East India Company, founded in 1600, began as a British trading venture in the Indian Ocean region. Its initial focus was on importing valuable spices, textiles, and other goods from the East Indies. Over time, the company established trading posts and factories in India, leading to its involvement in local politics and governance. By the mid-eighteenth century, the company effectively ruled large parts of India and became a significant political and economic power. However, its unchecked authority and exploitative practices led to social and political unrest. In 1858, the British Crown took control of India from the company, marking the end of its rule. The East India Company's evolution, from a trading entity to a quasi-governmental power, had a profound impact on India's history, ultimately paving the way for British colonial rule and, later, modern India's political landscape.

The East India Company, which once wielded immense power and influence over India, eventually faced economic troubles and was dissolved in 1874. It became a historical relic, fading into obscurity. However, its legacy remains significant. It played a pivotal role in shaping British colonialism and trade, and its activities laid the groundwork for the British Empire's presence in India. Today, the East India Company exists as a retail brand and a symbol of its historical legacy. It has rebranded itself as a luxury goods company, offering products such as teas, fine foods, and accessories, utilising its historical association to create a unique brand identity that combines the allure of the past with modern commerce.

keeping the spleen free of obstructions. Before this, coffee, which came from Arabia, had been widely drunk instead, and coffee houses had become a common feature in towns and cities.

The British East India Company held their first tea auction on 11 March 1679 at their headquarters in London, but tea was still seen as an exotic and expensive drink with medicinal values consumed by the wealthy. It was only in 1689 that China granted the British a trading post in the port of Canton (now Guangzhou), and thus England started importing tea directly from China.

The Opium Wars

Once the British became tea-obsessed, they began trading British silver with China in exchange for tea, as China effectively had a monopoly on the product. The trade continued until the British supply of silver became scarce in 1770, after which they started growing opium in India to trade instead. Britain controlled most of India at that time through the East India Company, giving them ample land to grow opium. In the words of Dr Rajen Barua, 'By [the] 1830s the British East India Company also had organised the first and most likely the biggest drug cartel in the world.'

While Britain was becoming addicted to tea, China was becoming addicted to the opium they traded it for. And Britain insisted that the Chinese pay for opium with British silver, so that they could, in turn, use that same silver to buy tea. The opium–silver–tea circulation became known as the Silver Triangle, and the continual circulation of the same silver progressively damaged the Chinese economy. At the same time the availability of opium was creating millions of addicts. China responded by banning opium, but the trade continued, with the

East India Company continuing to auction its opium to smaller traders, who smuggled it into China, even after the death penalty was introduced for opium traders in 1838.

In 1839, Chinese officials forced the Chief Superintendent of British Trade, Charles Elliot, to release British opium stocks held in Canton for destruction, and introduced a system of trade prohibiting merchants from bringing illegal goods into the country. This required merchants to sign a bond, which Elliot ordered them not to do, increasing the trade-related tensions. Around the same time, drunken British merchant sailors murdered a villager named Lin Weixi. Elliot refused a request from China to turn the sailors over to Chinese authorities. In retaliation, the Chinese blockaded Macau, where the British had been staying, causing them to be expelled and move to Hong Kong, as well as preventing food from being sold to the British. Elliot issued an ultimatum stating that, if the British were not allowed to trade for food with locals in Kowloon (the area north of Hong Kong), British ships would open fire on the port. The First Opium War broke out on 4 September 1839.

Britain won this war in 1842, leading to the Treaty of Nanking, which gave Hong Kong island to Britain, opened up five ports to British trade, allowing free British trade with any merchants in China, and forced China to pay damages for the destroyed opium. However, Britain demanded that the treaty be renegotiated as they wanted the opium trade to be legalised and the whole of China to be open to foreign trade. This is what led to the Second Opium War breaking out in 1856. China was defeated once again, ending in the Treaty of Tientsin, which gave Britain Kowloon. These two Opium Wars could just as well have been called the Tea Wars, as they were as much about the British obsession with tea as they were about China's dependence on opium.

Finding tea in Assam

Even before the Opium Wars began, the British had realised they needed another source of tea. In 1823 Robert Bruce, a Scottish explorer and merchant, discovered a plant resembling the tea plants found in China growing wild in the upper Brahmaputra Valley when he visited Rangpur, capital of the Ahom Kingdom in what is now Assam. He was in close contact with a local nobleman, Maniram Dutta, popularly known as Maniram Dewan, who introduced Bruce to a local Singpho chief, Bisa Gaum. Robert Bruce died soon afterwards in 1824, but his work was carried on by his brother, Charles Bruce.

Aided by a team of labourers, Charles Bruce cleared areas of land in Assam's harsh and hostile conditions, which are cold in winter and humid and hot in summer. Wild animals including tigers, elephants, wolves and snakes threatened the workers, but eventually the jungle was tamed and India's first tea plantations were established.

The Singpho chief was meant to be paid land rent by the East India Company. Annoyed when this payment was delayed, legend has it that Bisa Gaum slashed at the newly planted tea in anger, only realising later that the cut plants grew even better. According to the story, this initiated the practice of pruning. The estate where he cut the plants still exists and is called Bessakopie, which means 'where Bisa chopped off the tea plant'.

Bruce discovered that Chinese tea seedlings (*Camellia sinensis*) grew much less well than the indigenous variety (*Camellia assamica*), but nevertheless in 1835 he was able to send twelve cartons of newly grown tea to the Tea Committee in London, which was approved by the governor-general of India, Lord Auckland, and experts. The first consignment of Indian tea –

The Singpho centuries-old method of processing tea, 'dhooan chaang', is still used today. This method starts with roasting or pan-frying the tea leaves, then stuffing these leaves into bamboo hollows and leaving them to dry on a bamboo platform, called 'Dhuan-Chang' in Assamese, constructed above traditional wood-fired ovens. The hot smoke from the ovens dries the tea leaves over a period of around three months, imparting a smoky flavour.

forty-eight chests – arrived at London's Canary Wharf from Assam in 1839, and was declared to be wonderful by tea connoisseurs (the eight chests that were good, at least, as the rest had become mouldy). The London experts declared the tea 'satisfactory for a first experiment'.

However, the British tea experts still believed that the cultivated China tea or a China–Assam hybrid was far superior to the pure Assam variety, which they felt was too wild to be palatable. The British East India Company therefore planned an astounding plot to steal tea plants and tea seeds from China. In 1848, it sent a Scottish botanist called Robert Fortune to travel through China, cunningly disguised in traditional Chinese garb, with a long braid of dark hair sewn onto the nape of his neck. Fortune discovered that green and black tea come from the same plants, simply differing in the processing: green tea is unoxidised, while black tea is produced by oxidising the leaves. He stole more than 20,000 plants and seedlings, as well as poaching Chinese tea workmen, who returned with him to India.

Chinese seeds flourished in Indian soil, and tea plantations in India began to thrive. Eventually growers found that China–

Assam hybrid plants were less suited to the Assam environment, and substituted it with improved varieties of the native Assam plant. From then on Assam became the home of tea and the Assam Company, created in 1839, became the first commercial tea company in the world. Another company, called the Bengal Tea Association, was formed in Kolkata in 1839, with Willam Carr, William Princep and Dwarkanath Tagore (grandfather of Nobel Laureate Rabindranath Tagore) among the nine directors. The two companies soon merged under the Assam Company name, and it became the first joint stock company with shareholders in London and Kolkata. It still trades and operates today.

By 1860, Indian tea, whether grown from native Indian tea plants or seeds stolen from China, began to replace Chinese tea, and Britain was finally able to satisfy the national demand for tea with supplies grown within its own empire's borders. As Erica Rappaport writes in her book, *A Thirst for Empire*, 'on two sides of the world at the same time, Britons were making tea British . . . This act of appropriation reveals a complex dance in which the British contended with their desires, fears and fantasies about Asia.'

Assam and slave labour

At the time of writing, Assam contributes more than 50 per cent of India's tea production, and has more than a million tea workers in the organised sector, working in about 850 big estates. The tea belts of Brahmaputra and Barak valleys are home to more than 6 million people. Assam remains the single largest tea-growing region in the world, producing nearly 700 million kilograms of tea annually.

This gives an indication of the labour required to keep the tea industry operating, and it's worth touching on the complexities of that labour here, as it speaks to the historial, economic and colonial forces that influenced tea production. Because the British preference was initially for the Chinese tea plants, 'genuine' Chinese tea-growers seemed essential, thus the industry initially recruited Chinese workers. However, before growing and cultivation could begin, the planters needed to clear Assam's jungles, which required wearisome manual labour. Although the Chinese men had been hired to grow and process tea, not clear land, the scarcity of labour in the region meant that they were often expected to perform gruelling tasks, while physically debilitated in new surroundings and overwhelmed by disease and unfamiliar food. During the rains, many fell ill with malaria and other ailments, and lacking proper care, the attrition rate was high. The Assam Company returned many Chinese recruits to Kolkata, calling them 'turbulent, obstinate and rapacious'.

During the 1840s and 1850s, the Assam Company began recruiting from local groups in Upper Assam, paying them far lower wages than the Chinese workers. Under the direction of Charles Bruce, many were trained as taklars (tea-makers). Again, it was difficult to retain these workers and the planters put their perceived indolence down to easy access to opium, since it grew abundantly in their gardens. As historian Jayeeta Sharma writes, 'for colonial officials, opium was the definitive sign of a profligate native.'

The renewed quest for a more amenable worker led the British to search out the 'primitive virtues' of diligence and docility associated with some indigenous tribes, specifically the Kachari inhabitants of the Lower Assam districts of Kamrup, Lakhimpur, Darrang and Goalpara. Brian Hodgson,

Himalayan explorer and a British Political Officer in Nepal, was the first ethnographer to systematically study the Kacharis, whose long exposure to mountainous terrain made them more able to work in inhospitable climates, and who were more docile, as the 'labouring class' of the country. However, yet again, planters complained that they lacked the power to discipline these workers, who deserted after taking advances, and their ability to leave without notice enraged the colonial capital. It seemed that skilled Chinese, hard-working Kachari and the 'indolent' Upper Assamese were all equally ill-suited to the tea industry.

Thus began the search for yet another source of tea-worker, with primitivity as the driving factor. In the words of academic Anisha Bordoloi, this 'notion of "primitivity" was crucial in categorising a population in order to legitimise the differences between the ruler and the ruled, the coloniser and the colonised. Its creation was coterminous with the creation of colonial subjects and consolidation of empire in a frontier region like Assam.' It's hard not to conclude that the tea companies were deliberately looking for a workforce who could be more easily oppressed.

In colonial vocabulary, the labourers were called 'tea coolies'. Originally, coolies were the South Asian labourers recruited to Indian Ocean sugar plantations as replacements for African slaves during the British Empire's slave emancipation in the 1830s.* The majority belonged to tribal groups of Central and Eastern India, displaced peasant communities such as the Santhals, Oraons, Mundas, Kols, Gonds and Konds, who were

---

* In the words of historian Nitin Varma, '"Coolie" is a generic category for the "unskilled" manual labour . . . Coolie labour was often proclaimed as a deliberate compromise straddling the regimes of the past (slave labour) and the future (free labour).'

procured from Bengal, Orissa, Chota Nagpur, the United Provinces, the Central Provinces, Nepal and even as far as Madras and Bombay. Given the earlier occupation of these people as peasants in forested tracts, the planters assumed that these tribal communities would adapt to the work conditions in Assam and be fit for the laborious physical work required in the continuing clearing of the jungles along with the digging, hoeing and sowing activities that went into creating a plantation.

Thus started the indentured labour system of Assam, considered to be a less severe form of slavery, although in fact the lines were blurred and the 'coolies' were treated so badly that they often regarded Assam as 'the end of the world'. From 1860 to 1947, the planters transported 3 million labourers. Flogging and other measures were considered necessary to discipline the workforce, and, with no knowledge of the land, these 'coolies' had no way of escaping. From the 1860s, the British state worked closely with Assam planters to establish a regime of coolie indenture contracts buttressed by harsh penal legislation. They were locked in at night, living in the middle of remote, forested terrain, with little or no contact with local villagers, which made it impossible for them to escape. Rapes, flogging and other brutalities were committed on the 'coolie' women who were brought to the plantations with their families. The primary purpose of this intimidation was to create a sense of fear among the coolies and to keep them obedient. In Santhal, one of the main provinces the coolies came from, children learned to look upon Assam as a 'death trap' from where their ancestors had never returned.

And so the tea empire, with Assam at its heart, was built on the sweat and indentured labour of millions of tea labourers who were brought to Assam from all over India to work on the plantations. All this earned the tea industry the title of

'Planter's Raj', and early in the twentieth century there were increasing instances of coolie resistance, killings of workers as well as planters, and an all-India nationalist agitation against the indentured labour system spearheaded by Gandhi and C. F. Andrews, a priest and social reformer who became an advocate for Indian independence and a supporter and friend of Mahatma Gandhi, which finally led to the end of the system, between 1908 and 1926.

After independence in 1947, the descendants of Assam's indentured labourers renamed themselves the 'tea-tribe' or 'Adibasi' (literally meaning the 'original dweller', akin to the indigenous groups in tribal India), or 'baganiya' ('people of the garden'). But these new identities did not translate into social and economic change. In recent years, however, India has become a prominent contributor in producing Fair Trade-certified teas, whereby they are in compliance with the Fair Trade partnership that seeks respect for workers. Organisations such as the Ethical Tea Partnership are working in Assam and other tea-producing countries to improve the lives of people in tea communities. In Assam, through their partnership with UNICEF, the tea companies are working with organisations that aim to reduce child marriage and unsafe migration, as well as to improve living and working conditions on tea estates in Assam.

How tea came to Darjeeling and other regions

The *Camellia sinensis* plant brought by Robert Bruce from China, which did not flourish in Assam, seemed to thrive in the cooler, vertiginous environs of Darjeeling.

Planted at high elevation in northern India, the heart of the Eastern Himalayas, the Victorian 'hill town' Darjeeling today produces just a fraction of the world's tea, less than 1 per cent of India's total, but this tea is considered the best in the world. Darjeeling tea is a bright, amber-coloured brew with muscatel flavours, and has earned the nickname 'champagne of teas'.

It was first planted in 1841 by Dr Archibald Campbell, superintendent of the district, who was also an avid horticulturist. The first commercial tea plantation was then established in 1856, and by 1866 there were thirty-nine tea gardens in Darjeeling of 1,000 acres, producing a total crop of 21,000 kilograms of tea.

Seeing the success of the Darjeeling plantations, planters realised that tea could be cultivated in surrounding areas, such as Terai in the Himalayan foothills, and Dooars, where the Assamese tea bush seemed better suited. A tea plantation was set up in Kangra, at the foot of the Western Himalayas, and then in South India, in the Nilgiris, around the newly developed town known as Ooty (short for Ootacamund).

British consumption, independence and becoming 'swadeshi'

With all this tea being produced, the next necessity was to create, expand and maintain a thriving market of consumers. But who was to drink it all? After the Boston Tea Party in 1773, when 342 chests of tea belonging to the British East India Company were thrown from ships into Boston Harbour by American patriots protesting against the tax imposed by the British on tea, American consumption had reduced. Although Americans continued to smuggle tea into America, it was in very small quantities, and this ceased altogether during the American Civil War in the 1860s, when America ceased importing both tea and cotton. British Prime Minister William Pitt the Younger had removed the tax on tea in Britain in 1794, which had led to an expansion of the British market. By the 1890s, India and Ceylon had overtaken China in tea exports to Britain, but even then there was a limited number of people able to afford to brew the imported leaves.

Thus Britain looked at creating a market in India for the surplus tea. In the end, India would become both grower and consumer, but this took time and effort. Nowadays, it's hard to imagine the streets of India without chaiwalas on every corner, or entering someone's house without being offered chai, but there was a time, around a century ago, when few Indians drank tea. As journalist Vikram Doctor discovered, 'that time was within the memory of Prakash Tandon, the first Indian chairman of Hindustan Lever, who passed away [in 2004] at the age of 91. In his memoirs of growing up in an undivided Punjab he recalls that his great-uncle would drink a glass of milk, almond or fruit juice in the afternoons, but tea was never drunk except for medicinal purposes. The only people who drank tea in India were Europeans and the Indians influenced by them.' My grandmother recalls her own grandmother making tea on the stove in the village where she grew up, but this would have been in the early 1940s, just before independence, by which time the British had run their nationwide campaign to get Indians hooked on tea.

This campaign was launched in the early twentieth century, when the Indian Tea Market Expansion Board (ITMEB) gave away millions of cups of free tea to Indians across the country, sometimes from motorised 'tea vans'. Initially it was a drink for the Indian upper and middle classes in Kolkata, the colonial capital that had become the world's largest tea port. Slowly, the tea habit spread through India, but still it mostly existed in urban areas. Colourful posters and enamel placards put up in railway stations explained the process of infusing tea the 'correct' (that is, English) way. 'Demonstration teams' were sent to festivals and bazaars, and women-only teams to the inner quarters of conservative, purdah-observing households. The ITMEB also encouraged factory owners and managers to set up free or subsidised canteens offering an afternoon 'tea break' to workers, saying that this would result in more alertness and higher productivity.

After independence in 1947, tea estates passed from British to Indian hands. Part of the Indian independence movement had been the rejection of British-made goods, resulting in the boycotting and destruction of commodities such as textiles imported from Lancashire. The tea owners thus had the task of making tea-drinking 'swadeshi', meaning indigenous, or 'of the country', as well as convincing consumers that it was conducive to health. According to historian Philip Lutgendorf, 'the publicity adopted the nationalist rhetoric of the independence movement to champion tea as India's "national beverage" that (like a "national language", "national costume", "national song", etc.) could potentially unify the subcontinent's diverse religious, linguistic and caste groups.'

Annada Munshi (considered by many as the father of Indian art) produced a poster in 1947, the year of independence, heralding this transition, with a chaste, sari-clad 'Mother India', seated behind the iconic charkha (spinning wheel) of Gandhian homespun cotton, enjoying a cup of tea, with the announcement that 'tea IS 100% SWADESHI'. The tea owners also adopted the rhetoric of 'national integration' (a government slogan of the post-independence period), such as the Bengali blender A. Tosh & Sons, which declared 'Diverse castes, diverse creeds – but about Tosh tea, all are of one mind!' and the

Gujarati tea dealer Wagh Bakri, which aired a television advert in which tea-sipping singers in costumes representing different parts of India chanted, 'Diverse ornaments, diverse costumes, in name, so many states. But, with just one sip, a nation is forged,' culminating in an image of mingling streams of chai forming the spokes of the dharma-wheel emblem on India's flag.

The Indianisation of tea, which is the addition of spices and milk, along with what historian Arun Chatterjee calls the 'lassification' of tea (making it thick and creamy like a lassi), had already started from 1910. But this amplified after independence, as did the number of chaiwalas. As for the marriage of

tea and spices creating chai, this came about through waves of experimentation between the First World War and the 1930s, with chaiwalas trying to differentiate themselves with their spice blends. In the process, they discovered a way to make bitter tea more palatable and, indeed, cheaper, as milk and spices were inexpensive compared to tea leaves. Using less tea was also an act of rebellion against the British, because before independence tea profits went directly to the colonial rulers.

As chai became the drink of rich and poor alike, steel and glass chai cups started replacing the old colonial-style porcelain artefacts. Tea-drinking spread from urban to rural India and village tea culture mushroomed. It was no longer the drink of the elites, but a drink that crossed all stratas and classes, brought communities together and became truly Indian, or swadeshi. In less than fifty years, British tea had morphed into Indian chai and was thus a marker of the new India.

The demand for tea gained further momentum in India in the 1950s and 1960s after the introduction of CTC (Crush, Tear, and Curl) Tea, a method of manufacturing tea that revolutionised the Indian tea industry and made tea much more affordable for the Indian masses. The process of producing tea had been very labour intensive until this machinery was introduced, but this process, where dried-up tea leaves are passed through a series of cylindrical rollers with sharp teeth that crush, tear and curl the leaves, producing small pellets of tea leaves, changed that. These pellets were then fermented to bring out the flavour or tannins,˙ resulting in teas of deep colour and flavour, able to blend well with milk.

---

* Tannins are a kind of plant compound found in tea and other plant foods and drinks. They are responsible for giving tea its dry, somewhat bitter and astringent flavour and providing colour in certain types of tea.

People in rural India, dhabas and chaiwalas didn't have the time or luxury to brew loose-leaf tea in pots and preferred tea dust, which is the smallest size of tea made during the tea-manufacturing process (see page 47). And so, 'dust tea' was born, with 'Kora' as the first brand to be introduced by Brooke Bond in paper-form packets. Certain countries, such as Ireland, also preferred smaller tea-leaf particles for rapid brewing, as did the Americans, for filling teabags. This is why the CTC machines played such an important role in speeding up the process and making it more accessible to the masses. As to exactly when a roadside and railway chaiwala realised that they could boil all the ingredients in a single vessel, rather than all the fuss of preheating the tea in a porcelain pot and setting out a separate creamer and sugar bowl, is very unclear, but this switch was very important in the creation and definition of Indian chai. So tea became more available, affordable and popular, rapidly transforming into the ubiquitous Indian beverage it is today.

According to industry insiders, the availability of CTC was the most important factor driving the massive growth in consumption that led, by the end of the century, to the domestic market accounting for some 75 per cent of India's annual crop of more than 800 million kilograms; a reversal from 1947, when more than 70 per cent of India's annual tea crop, then the biggest in the world, was still destined for foreign throats. Tea does not belong to Britain, nor did Britain find it, but it is through the Empire, and the East India Company in particular, that tea, made from plants first found in China, has now become the most widely consumed beverage in the world next to water.

How and where tea is grown today

The varying climates in which tea is grown in India – Assam, Darjeeling, Nilgiris, Kangra Valley and Dooars – give each tea its own distinct flavour and character. The rich, green heartlands of the tea-growing industry, blooming with natural beauty, spectacular views and jungle wildlife, are intrinsic to the diverse landscape of India. The Indian tea journey is one that a traveller can now take. The tea plantations are often remote and thus more like self-contained villages or townships, but there are now boutique hotels and home stays to be found in plantations across India, which can provide a unique insight into the production of tea, the people who work there, and, with that, a renewed appreciation for this fascinating drink that has played such a key role in historical events and become our daily cup.

Coming from the Tibetan glaciers, the Brahmaputra river travels along the edges of many of these plantations. The river's name means 'Son of Lord Brahma, the Creator' and it is the only 'male' river in India, a country where rivers are always worshipped as a devi (goddess). It is also the second-largest river in India. There are beautiful waterfalls, trails, river rafting and horse riding to be enjoyed too, as well as wildlife in the national parks, and so a trip to the plantations will provide a very different experience of India, steeped in nature and the outdoors.

The larger tea estates sprawl out over hundreds of hectares of land, with perfect rows of tea bushes stretching into the horizon – a landscape as immaculate as it is silent. In the morning, though, in the words of writer Rekha Sarin, 'a ripple of voices and jingle of bangles fill the air as women set off towards their assigned tea leaf plucking areas.' And it is these women, the tea pluckers who weave through the rows of tea bushes with cloth hampers of wicker baskets on their backs, who are the backbone of the abundant tea estates and of their families. They swiftly and adeptly snap the 'two leaves and a bud' that makes for excellent teas; for other teas, they might pluck three, four or five leaves. A picker harvests almost 2,000–4,000 stems for a single kilogram of green leaf which, after being processed in the factory, would yield approximately 215 grams of made tea, depending on the leaf variety.

The different flushes of tea ❦ The quality, colour and strength of tea are affected by numerous seasonal factors, in the same way that the quality of wine is affected by climate, rainfall and sun exposure. Tea is harvested all year around, but has various 'flushes', which means that the same tea plant produces different types and flavours of tea depending on the season. Between the flushes are resting or dormant periods, called the bhanji.

Assam and Darjeeling have four flushes, called the First Flush, Second Flush, Monsoon Flush and Autumn Flush. The most sought after Darjeeling tea is the First Flush, making this the most expensive of all Darjeeling teas; and the most popular Assam tea is the Second Flush, making this the most expensive Assam tea.

Assam ❦ Tea from Assam is widely used by those who prefer strong tea, either alone or with milk and sugar; the addition of milk and sugar does not weaken the strength of the tea. Assam is also the single largest tea-growing region in the world.

The First Flush is made with the earliest spring shoots and buds picked from tea bushes in late March. This First Flush is plucked for eight to ten weeks and the resulting teas have a fresh, flowery character with a hint of green in their appearance. These tea leaves are used in blends and as breakfast teas, their high levels of tannins providing a good amount of energy for the morning.

The Second Flush is picked during the summer months, mid-May to mid-July, and this is when tea is considered to be in its prime, with a more robust taste, rich aroma and a somewhat malty flavour. The heavy rains and humidity at this time of year result in a prolific yield and so almost 75 per cent of Assam teas are produced during this season.

The Monsoon Flush is in July and September, the heaviest plucking months. While the Second Flush tea has a saffron hue, tea picked in the monsoon season is a little less bright in colour when brewed.

Lastly, the Autumn Flush appears as the weather becomes cooler. The excess moisture in the soil becomes absorbed into the shoots and leaves and thus dilutes the flavour of the tea, though it has a rich, earthy flavour. Therefore, these teas are used to make blends.

Darjeeling ✍ Darjeeling is nestled high in the Himalayas at the northernmost tip of West Bengal, overlooking the magnificent Kanchenjunga mountain, one of the highest in the Himalayas, which is shrouded in a cold mist most of the year. Its scenic glory, with mountain slopes and hills covered in wild flowers, makes it a great tourist destination.

Darjeeling tea, with its light, floral and fruity flavour, is considered the champagne of teas, and is produced in the crisp, clean mountain air of some eighty-seven estates that lie 700–7,000 feet above sea level.

Darjeeling tea is more expensive because it is more exclusive and rare, accounting for less than 1 per cent of all Indian teas. It takes about 22,000 young shoots to make 1 kilogram. The state's high altitude means that it has a much shorter tea season than Assam too, with the tea plants going into hibernation for a few months during the winter months, usually November to February.

Darjeeling's First Flush begins in March and April, just after the spring rains. First Flush Darjeeling teas are considered some of the finest, they have a delicate and flowery character, and are best enjoyed without milk.

The Second Flush teas are picked in May and June; they have a more mature, fruity and bold flavour with a deeper amber colour, and are better as an afternoon or evening tea. Some of the teas from this flush are called Muscatel, because their intense aroma and flavour is evocative of Muscat grapes. Tea lovers in Europe like to have this tea with cream and sugar.

The Monsoon Flush is picked in the rains of July, August and September, resulting in the darkest-coloured teas, which fare well in blends and teabags.

Lastly, the Autumn Flush is picked during October and November and has large leaves that have a much stronger taste than even monsoon teas.

South India ➤ The Nilgiris and the Western Ghats are entirely different from the Himalayan plantations. The hills have a subtropical setting and there are no seasonal flushes, rather tea grows and is plucked all year around. The terrains here are home to the shola forests and abundant water resources through rivers, streams and rainfall.

Overall, the teas are strong yet subtle, lying somewhere between the Assam and Darjeeling varieties, with tastes ranging from floral to nutty. The tea plantations in the south spread over the states of Tamil Nadu, Kerala and parts of Karnataka, and thus the entire region has the highest yield in India, contributing 17 per cent of India's total output.

Together, the teas from South India have a whole variety of characters due to the variations in terrain, soil and climate in the region: darker and stronger teas from Ooty in the Nilgiris, full-bodied teas with an orange-gold colour from Munnar, teas with medium and balanced characters from Chikmagalur, and mellow and mild tea from from Wayanad and Nelliyampathy. Other tea regions in the south include Anamalais, Coonoor, Idukki, High Wavys and Coorg, some of which are also coffee-growing districts.

Other tea-growing areas ✎ Aside from the main tea belts of Assam, Darjeeling and South India, there are some smaller areas located mainly in the foothills of the Himalayas, in the north-east, north and north-west.

The Dooars region lies just below Darjeeling. Its name means 'doors' in Bengali, Assamese and Nepali, and it's named so because it is the gateway to the north-east and Bhutan. The Dooars comprises the district of Jalpaiguri, West Bengal, along with a small part of Coochbehar District. The land has rhinos, forests and streams and produces teas rather like those from Assam: strong, good for blending and great with milk.

Another tea-growing region is the Kangra Valley in Himachal Pradesh. His Holiness the 14th Dalai Lama also resides in the Kangra Valley, in a town called McLeod Ganj near Dharamshala, nestled in the laps of the Himalayan mountain range, which also has some tea gardens. The tea here has floral notes, with a sweet aftertaste. 'I think it's the chants of the mornings that brings a certain harmony in the region,' says Anamika Singh, a tea sommelier and manufacturer living in Dharamshala, who is co-founder of Anandini Himalaya Tea.

Tea was first cultivated in Kangra Valley around the same time as in Darjeeling, although the area was struck by an earthquake in 1905 that crippled Kangra's tea industry for years afterwards. In the past three decades, however, production has increased and tea tourism is beginning to gain ground, with tea estates offering factory tours and home stays.

East of the holy pilgrimage town of Haridwar, up in the Kumaon Hills, there are small tea gardens in the Kasauni district, a hill station in Uttarakhand famous for its panoramic view of various Himalayan peaks. The tea plantations scattered over an area of 208 hectares are known to produce some of the richest qualities of tea.

Leaf to cup ᔕ The journey of tea leaves from the freshly plucked evergreen leaves to the twisted, dry, black or deep-green leaves which unfurl in hot water and release their delicate colours and aromas is a lengthy process with various steps, from growing and plucking the leaf, the production process, tea-tasting and then on to tea auctions. There are three main manufacturing systems: the first stops the oxidation process of the green leaf as soon it arrives in the factory, resulting in green tea; the second is partial oxidation resulting in Oolong tea; and the third produces black tea, where the leaf is fully oxidised, from which two teas can be made: Orthodox, which looks like twisted long leaf, and CTC, or Crush, Tear, and Curl, where the leaves look like short, tightly curled pellets. The production process of tea has progressed significantly – factories today have sophisticated computer-controlled machinery, and strict hygiene controls are in place.

Plucking – The process starts with plucking tea leaves, mostly done by hand, picking a terminal bud and two young leaves.

Once the tea arrives at the factory, having been transported in a three-tiered trailer to protect the shoots, a leaf sample is weighed.

Withering – This step is to reduce the moisture content in the leaves to make them more malleable by putting them into large withering troughs, which fan hot air. It can take twelve to twenty hours to wither the leaves sufficiently, depending on the temperature of the air as well as the thickness of leaf. This process causes physical and chemical changes in the leaf, which not only make it more malleable but intensify the volatile compounds, such as caffeine and polyphenols, which will determine the quality of the tea. In the early years, the leaves were withered by being spread on tats (wired shelves,) in covered sheds open on all sides, called chung houses. During this process of withering, 25–70 per cent of the moisture, depending on the attributes aimed at, is extracted from the leaf, making them soft and pliable for further processing.

Rolling/CTC – At this stage, if producing the popular CTC teas, the withered leaves are put into machines in which big rollers moving at a high speed shred the leaves and reduce their size. If making Orthodox tea, however, 'rolling' takes place, so that the leaf cells rupture to release juices. This step, which was once done manually and was incredibly laborious, is now mechanized: the leaves are fed through rollers into a machine to break up the leaf cells, essentially separating the bud, first leaf, second leaf and longer leaf. The leaves then go through sets of three or more rollers placed close together and revolving at different speeds, a process which crushes, tears and curls the leaf, hence the name CTC. The leaves will emerge as tightly curled pellets. In both these methods of production, the juices and enzymes originally separated in the cells of the leaf are now mixed. Orthodox rolling can take up to three hours, whereas CTC takes only ten minutes. Darjeeling produces only 'orthodox' or green tea, while all other areas from Assam to Kerala produce mostly CTC.

Fermentation/oxidation – It is this part of the process, oxidation, which is often referred to as fermentation in the tea industry, where the coloured compounds are formed giving the leaf a dark copper tone. The leaves are spread out on the floor or in a fermenting machine for one to three hours and left to allow oxidisation or fermentation in a cool atmosphere. This allows a series of chemical reactions to take place, such as the chlorophyll breaking down, which is begun when the leaf is broken in the roller. This releases the tannins, and the leaf can then develop its distinct flavour.

Firing/drying – This final stage, to finish the tea for sale, is to pass the leaves through a dryer, which blows hot air at temperatures ranging from 85°C to 130°C (185°F to 260°F). This stops oxidation and can take around twenty minutes, resulting in a very reduced moisture content. In the early years, dryers and heaters were housed in one unit and intense heat radiated from wood- or coal-fired stoves.

Sorting and grading – To sort tea leaves into particle sizes they are sent through sifters with different meshes, separating out the bigger leaves, after which the leaves are sorted into three main grades indicating leaf size known as broken, fannings and dust. The dust comes from the smallest of these leaves. Broken grades are then sorted again for premium and secondary grading. After this, the tea is packed into jute bags and woven sacks, with high-quality CTC teas sometimes vacuum packed to retain freshness. The packing is important as there should be no invasion of moisture, which is the greatest enemy to tea, as it will result in the degeneration of flavour. It may take as long as six months, for example, for a Second Flush tea plucked in May or June be available for consumption, and even longer if it is exported.

Tasting and assessing – The quality of the tea is now assessed by the expert taster, giving their final verdict on the quality and distinction between ordinary, fine and superlative teas. 'In a nutshell,' says Akhil Sapru, vice chairman of J Thomas & Co Pvt Ltd, the world's largest and oldest tea auctioneer, 'you have to look at how the (tea) leaf looks, how the infusion looks, and then how it tastes, how brisk the cup is, how much flavour there is to the cup, how is the 'body' in it?' Sapru, along with his fellow tea tasters, sample up to 2,000 cups a day from rows of the brew assembled in a long tea-tasting hall, to determine the quality, price and the markets they could sell each tea in.

Spices and Ayurveda ᴄ⌐ Before we move on to the ingredients used in today's tea blends, I'd like to touch on Kadha, a traditional Ayurvedic drink made from a blend of herbs and spices boiled in hot water (for a recipe, see page 134) – a tea without tea. Ayurveda is one of the world's oldest medical systems, a holistic tradition dating back 5,000 years. The word 'Ayurveda' translates as 'the science of life', and it is a healing system that originated in India around 5,000 years ago, but is still relevant today, based as it is on the principles of nature. The foundation of Ayurveda is living in tune with natural rhythms, supporting your digestion through food, movement and rest, and thus living in optimal health.

Each spice used in kadha (also known in some parts of India as kashayam) – usually ginger, cinnamon, cardamom, black pepper, tulsi, turmeric and cloves, although the blend depends on the practitioner – is known to have medicinal properties. Kadha is particularly used to aid digestion, boost metabolism as well as immunity, and relieve cold and flu symptoms. The ancient texts of Ayurveda explain the benefits of the herbs and spices, all considered powerful plant medicines. If you research any of the spices online today, you'll find pages and pages of information. We know more now than ever before as modern science proves and expands on the science behind this ancient wisdom.

As globalisation continues to bring cultures and customs closer together, kadha is increasingly becoming a popular drink beyond India's borders. The same could be said about Ayurveda, with more and more Ayurvedic practitioners in the West and the increasing popularity of learning about Ayurvedic cooking, foods and the principles of digestion, as well as increasing awareness about treating the root causes of disease and illness, rather than only treating the symptoms.

Chai Ingredients

The tea leaves you use, the spices you choose, the milk you enjoy, how milky or watery you like your hot drinks, and your palate for sweetness will all create your own individual chai. Simmering the tea and spices for a while will enhance the flavour of both, deepening the colour of the brew and thus making the chai more kadak, or strong. I personally love more spice and fewer tea leaves, while my parents, like most Gujaratis, need tea to be kadak and taste like proper tea, so it really is all about how you like it. If there's one thing I've realised from making chai over the years, it is that letting the chai simmer and then double-boiling it – by which I mean letting the tea rise to the top, then reducing the heat, and doing this twice, even thrice – makes all the difference to how strong the spices taste and how well they become assimilated. Do this right, and when you sip the chai, there's a smoothness to the spices, and you'll feel the fire at the back of your throat with each mouthful, especially if the spice blend contains ginger and pepper, and the spices will be so well combined in the chai that it is hard to tell which spices have been used.

As to which spices I use for my chai, I love to mix it up – sometimes just my mum's chai masala mix, sometimes I'll add grated ginger, at other times, I'll grind a couple of cardamom pods in a pestle and mortar to make a purely elaichi (cardamom) chai, and when I feel like something calming, I'll add saffron or even nutmeg. For me, chai is all about the spices. The spices are my medicine cabinet, what I turn to every single day, in all my cooking and drinks. I carry a small pot of ginger powder with me most days to stir into hot water, and sometimes a mixture of spices including fennel and cumin seeds. I'll keep a clove in my mouth if I'm feeling nauseous or have toothache, I carry my own chai blend (Chai by Mira) to have with hot milk or with my coffee, and when I travel, I carry a jar of various spices. It doesn't simply enhance a cup of tea, it makes it!

Milk

Milk is now a staple ingredient in making a cup of chai, although it only started being used in the early 1900s. It seems that the addition of milk originated in Gujarat and Bengal, where chai-walas had access to good-quality milk. Of course, adding milk, sugar and spices is also cost effective, as the tea leaves were the most expensive ingredient, so adding other ingredients brought down the overall cost by diluting the tea.

In India, chai is traditionally made with buffalo milk, as it is thicker and creamier than cow's milk; however, cow's milk is also widely used today. Chai is boiled with water and milk, and while the exact proportion of water and milk does vary, it is around half of each, but some do add more milk to make it creamier. The milk is also usually added after the tea and spices have been boiled in water. There are a few reasons for this, such as rehydrating the spices properly, but it is especially important to do this if using fresh ginger, as ginger has an enzyme that can curdle milk between 60°C and 70°C (140°F and 158°F), thus boiling the ginger in water first, along with any other spices and the tea leaves, before adding milk, will prevent this from happening.

Whole milk is said to bring out the richness of all the spices. However, in many of the hotels and cafés in India and elsewhere (although not from many authentic chaiwalas!), you can opt for chai made with non-dairy milks. And you can certainly make your own brew of masala chai at home with whichever milk you prefer.

In terms of flavour, soy-milk chai has a wholesome consistency and a nuttier flavour, which I love for chai. Coconut milk is also thick and has a natural sweetness, while oat milk is creamier and probably tastes the most similar to whole milk. Almond milk is possibly the lightest milk in terms of consistency, but still delicious.

Tea leaves

Any good black loose-leaf tea, for example Assam or Darjeeling, can be used for making chai. The important thing is that it needs to have good depth of flavour and colour, so that the taste of the tea really comes through.

While teabags are more convenient than loose-leaf tea, because you need not worry about straining the brewed tea, you are compromising on the quality and flavour. Most teabags are filled with the left-over dust from broken tea leaves, i.e. what remains after the quality leaves have been used for loose tea, hence it is generally lower grade. Loose-leaf teas are generally fresher and more aromatic. Teabags are also, in most cases, too small to allow leaves the space to unfurl, and this is another reason why they are generally filled with 'tea dust'.

When you steep larger or whole leaves, the essential oils and minerals they contain are released into the water, whereas tea dust lacks much of these oils and aroma in the first place, hence you get fewer nutrients and much less flavour all round. With loose-leaf tea, the leaves 'bloom' and are in contact with more of the water, providing a stronger flavour. You are also often paying more for teabags, as compared to loose leaf, and while teabags are designed to be thrown away after using once, with loose tea you can brew the leaves several times. However, there is, of course, a whole range of teabags out there, and the high-end, good-quality teabags are larger and do use whole leaves. So make sure you pick the right ones.

Loose-leaf teas with smaller, broken leaves will also infuse better than full-leaf teas, so try to use varieties that are processed using the CTC (Crush, Tear, and Curl) method. As with many ingredients, organic teas are generally more flavourful than non-organic varieties, as well as often being healthier and better for the environment.

The benefits of tea

As we've seen, it's no exaggeration to say that tea has been the cause of wars. Worldwide, our addiction to tea and coffee draws light to the psychosensory qualities of these beverages, and how their chemical make-up alters consciousness. As Michael Pollan writes in his book *This is Your Mind on Plants*, 'what really commends these beverages to us is their association not with wood smoke or stone fruit or biscuits, but with the experience of well-being – of euphoria – they reliably give us'. There are drinks that taste far better than tea and coffee, so why is it that we have tea culture and coffee culture, and there are shops and cafés dedicated to both?

A study published in the journal *Psychopharmacology* found that people who drink black tea are able to de-stress more quickly than those who drink a tea substitute; the scientists found that tea has an effect on stress hormone levels in the body. Professor Andrew Steptoe of the UCL Department of Epidemiology and Public Health, conducted with colleagues a study which suggests that 'drinking black tea may speed up our recovery from the daily stresses in life. Although it does not appear to reduce the actual levels of stress we experience, tea does seem to have a greater effect in bringing stress hormone levels back to normal. This has important health implications, because slow recovery following acute stress has been associated with a greater risk of chronic illnesses such as coronary heart disease.' According to Steptoe, the ingredients of tea are so chemically complex that scientists don't know which are responsible for the effects on stress recovery and relaxation: 'ingredients such as catechins, polyphenols, flavonoids and amino acids have been found to have effects on neurotransmitters in the brain, but we cannot tell from this research which ones produced the differences'.

Herbs and spices

There is something intensely comforting about inhaling the aroma of spices as they boil in a pot of chai. Each spice is different, as is each spice blend, both in aroma and flavour. Add sugar to the brew and a blend of sweetness and spice will waft in the air. Spices are the foundation of Indian cuisine and, indeed, Indian drinks. How can one masala chai taste so different from another by simply using a different spice? Cardamom can be warm and floral, ginger strong and spicy, cinnamon adds a gentle yet fiery sweetness, pepper is pungent and hot. Different combinations and permutations of spices can make a cup of chai taste entirely different.

It seems there is a scientific reason for this. Professor Ganesh Bagler, who is now considered the pioneer of computational gastronomy in India and who co-authored a study by the premier institute for higher studies in India, described spices as 'the molecular fulcrum of Indian food.' Indian cuisine is characterised by a unique contrasting pattern of food pairing. Combining ingredients with very different flavours in one recipe is what gives Indian cuisine a very distinct taste. Breaking down a collection of the late, celebrated Indian chef Tarla Dalal's recipes, Bagler realised that spices form the basis of food-pairing in Indian cuisine. Having divided various foods into twenty-six categories – vegetables, dairy, lentils, meats, etc. – he saw that mixing up these ingredients in any combination did not cause too much of a shift in flavour, but when the spices were shuffled, the taste changed entirely. And this therefore explains why using different spices and different spice blends can make one chai taste so different from another.

In addition to giving chais their delicious and distinctive flavours, herbs and spices boost the digestion and the metabolism, among other healthy properties. Ginger and cinnamon, for example, lower blood-sugar levels, and ginger is anti-inflammatory. Cardamom supports the immune system and improves blood circulation. Cloves are a natural painkiller and alleviate nausea. Tea itself is rich in antioxidants, helping to protect cells from the free radicals that can lead to heart disease, cancer, Alzheimer's, Parkinson's and other ailments.

Many of the spices are also effective in promoting gut health, and because of the close connection between gut and brain, we know that a healthy gut has a positive effect on our mood and mental function. According to Ayurveda (see page 48), digestion is central to good health. In fact, diseases and imbalances in the body can often be traced back to digestion. Ayurveda comes from two Sanskrit words: 'ayur', meaning 'life', and 'veda', meaning 'knowledge' or 'scripture', and thus it translates to 'knowledge of life' or 'scripture of life'.

When the food we eat is not digested properly, the ama – the by-product or toxins of poor digestion and metabolism – builds up, blocking the flow of nutrients to different parts of the body and weakening the immune system. A key element of Ayurveda is using herbs and spices to enhance digestion and to maintain balance in the body. They also help remove accumulated ama. Spices and herbs should be taken consistently and daily, as they work gradually, with the benefits stacking up over time. Adding spices to your chai, having them in hot water, and, above all, cooking with spices, are all great ways to use spices daily and so to ensure that you feel the effects over time.

Furthermore, since one of the basic tenets of Ayurveda is to try to include all six tastes in each meal – sweet, sour, salty, bitter, pungent and astringent – spices are a great way of doing this.

The spices

Cardamom is a herbal, peppery and slightly sweet spice from the ginger family. Green cardamom (there is also black cardamom) is the third most expensive spice after saffron and vanilla. However, saffron is used very sparingly – a few strands can be enough for a dessert or a chai – whereas you need a little more cardamom to bring out the flavour. Cardamom is the product of a very labour-intensive process and needs to be harvested by hand, which is what makes it more expensive; it currently trades at around $9 per kilo, whereas cinnamon, for example, sells for $2–4 per kilo.

India is the world's largest producer of cardamom, and it grows in abundance in the evergreen forests of the Western Ghats of South India. References to it in ancient Sanskrit texts date back 5,000 years to the Late Vedic period. Ground cardamom is used in many desserts and is certainly one of the essential ingredients, along with ginger, in making chai. Cardamom helps with digestion issues, improves mood and soothes a sore throat or cough. When using cardamom in chai, it's best to crush or open the pods, so that the flavour will infuse into the chai properly. You could use a pestle and mortar to do this, or simply crush the pods on a chopping board with something heavy.

Cinnamon comes from the inner bark of the cinnamon tree, which is dried to make cinnamon sticks, which are tan-coloured and often tightly rolled pieces of bark. Cinnamon is indigenous to Sri Lanka and south-west India, and it is one of the oldest-known of all spices, mentioned in the Bible and in Sanskrit texts. True cinnamon comes from *Cinnamomum verum*, 'a medium-sized, evergreen tree with glossy three-veined leaves and small white flowers. The fruits are oblong and dark purple, resembling small acorns.' It has a subtly sweet, warming and earthy aroma, a spicy and sweet flavour and is used mostly in desserts and drinks, but also in some savoury dishes. Cinnamon is packed with antioxidants, it has anti-inflammatory properties and helps to regulate blood-sugar levels, making it beneficial for those at risk of and living with diabetes. Brain benefits associated with cinnamon consumption in humans include reduced inflammation, improved memory, increased attention and enhanced cognitive processing.

Cloves are the dried, aromatic flower buds of the tropical clove tree. With a distinctive strong and spicy flavour, they are known for their medicinal properties and high nutritional content, containing manganese and vitamins C and K. Cloves can help with a range of health issues from stomach ulcers and tooth pain to nasal congestion.

Cumin has a rustic, earthy flavour and, according to Ayurveda, is a cooling spice which aids digestion, can ease stomach pain, relaxes the muscles and purifies the skin and blood. In Indian cooking, cumin seeds are used both whole as the base, or 'tadka', of curry, and are also ground into a fine powder to be stirred into cooking or used in making lassi. Sautéing and roasting the seeds brings out the flavour.

Fennel seeds have a warm aniseed flavour and can help with bloating and constipation, normalise blood pressure and prevent bad breath. Indians chew on these after a meal, and you'll often find a bowl of fennel seeds at restaurants in India, sometimes sugar-coated. Drinking fennel tea can also help with digestion.

Ginger, whose scientific name is *Zingiber officinale*, comes from the underground stem, or rhizome, of the ginger plant. Warm, spicy and zesty, it has a wide range of health benefits, from reducing inflammation to soothing an upset stomach and relieving nausea. Its origin can be traced back to Southeast Asia, particularly India and China, where it has been used in traditional medicine for thousands of years. The ancient Greeks and Romans also used ginger for medicinal purposes, as did the Chinese and Indians. Today, ginger is used all over the world as a spice and a medicine. It is also high in antioxidants, which can help protect against chronic diseases such as cancer and heart disease. Additionally, ginger shows effective glycaemic control properties in diabetes, and a study on brain health demonstrates that ginger may enhance both attention and cognitive processing in middle-aged women.

Holy basil or **tulsi** is a medicinal herb that is sacred in India and in Ayurveda. It is considered to be an adaptogen, a herbal pharmaceutical that helps the body to resist stress. It also decreases anxiety and adrenal fatigue, and has antioxidant and antimicrobial properties.

Lemongrass is the stalk of a grass that grows in tropical climates. It has a citrusy aroma and flavour, with a hint of mint, and has long been used in traditional medicines. It is considered to be a calming and cooling herb in Ayurveda. Lemongrass tea is a diuretic, flushing toxins from the body. Lemongrass oil is used in aromatherapy to help treat headaches, body aches and exhaustion.

Nutmeg is made from the seeds of a tropical evergreen tree. After harvesting the fruit, the seed is dried for a period of weeks, to produce the spice. Its origin can be traced back to Indonesia, where it was first cultivated and traded by Arab and Indian merchants. Nutmeg was considered a valuable and rare commodity, one of the rarest spices in the world, and many believed it was a cure for the Plague. At the time, it was only cultivated in the Banda Islands, known as the Spice Islands, ten islands in the Indonesian archipelago. In the early seventeenth century, the Dutch East India Company (VOC) seized the islands from the Portuguese and moved to monopolise the trade with what Oliver Thring, writing for the *Guardian*, described as 'paranoid brutality, banning the export of the trees, drenching every nutmeg in lime before shipping to render it infertile, and imposing the death penalty on anyone suspected of stealing, growing or selling nutmegs elsewhere'. The Dutch, in fact, perpetrated a massacre. Control of the islands was a source of conflict, especially between the English and the Dutch, both sides wanting to protect their monopoly over certain spices. Eventually, the Dutch ceded control of Manhattan to the British in exchange for control of the last nutmeg-producing island under British rule. Nutmeg now grows in China, Malaysia, India, Sri Lanka and even South America.

In traditional medicine, nutmeg was used to treat various ailments such as digestive problems, insomnia and anxiety. With a warm and slightly nutty flavour, it is used in desserts, curries and drinks such as chai. Nutmeg has sleep-inducing effects, is high in antioxidants and is antibacterial. Studies have also suggested that nutmeg may be beneficial in reducing the symptoms of chronic pain conditions such as arthritis and neuropathic pain. It is even used in some dental products. When taken in large quantities, however, nutmeg can have psychoactive effects, which come from the presence of a chemical called myristicin. Nutmeg intoxication may produce symptoms similar to those of anticholinergic poisoning, including delirium and tremors.

Pepper is known as the King of Spices and economically, it is the most important and most widely used spice crop in the world. In ancient Egypt, when the mummified body of the Pharaoh was laid to rest in the pyramids, it was black pepper, along with gold and silver, that was kept adjacent to the body, in the belief that pepper would be of use even in the afterlife. The Bible, the Koran and the Vedas all mention pepper, the ancient Indian texts the *Ashtangahridaya* and the *Samhitas* explain the use of pepper in medical formulations, and in India today a herbal tincture called trikatu, containing black pepper, long pepper and ginger, is widely prescribed in Ayurvedic medicine.

Peppercorns are berries from the plant *Piper nigrum*. Although 'nigrum' means 'black', white pepper comes from the same plant. The difference depends on when the berries are picked and dried. Black pepper is harvested when the berries are still green, while white pepper is picked later, when the berries have turned from green to red. Black peppercorns are picked when almost ripe and sun-dried, which turns the outer layer black. To produce white peppercorns, this outer layer is removed before or after drying, leaving only the inner seed. White pepper is hotter and earthier than black pepper, with a less complex flavour. Both types can boost the metabolism, help soothe coughs and colds and improve digestion.

Pepper is what pulled the world to India and, in the words of Indian agronomist Kodoth Prabhakaran Nair, 'in hindsight, what is most astonishing is how a trade war in pepper between the Dutch and the British led to the establishment of the British Empire on the Indian subcontinent'. It was the lure of the spice trade that led Vasco da Gama, the great Portugese explorer, to discover the sea route to India and land on the Malabar Coast on 20 May 1498. This led to the Portugese domination of Kerala, the state which became the cradle of world pepper. This changed with the arrival of the Dutch in the first quarter of the seventeenth century.

And so this one spice redefined the history of India and could be considered the precursor to chai, the reason the British came to India and thus what brought about the creation and proliferation of the tea industry.

The medicinal benefits of pepper, as shown in the Ayurvedic texts and Chinese medicine, is gaining traction and being explained by modern science. As author Marjorie Shaffer remarks in her book *Pepper*, 'scientists in the United States, Britain and Italy have tested pepper's potency as an anti-inflammatory and antimicrobial agent, an anticancer therapy, preservative, insecticide, antioxidant, as a treatment for vitiligo and more. Some studies suggest that pepper could improve mood and slim the waistline. In China, chemicals derived from pepper are incorporated into medicines to treat epileptic seizures in children.'

Saffron is produced from the stigmas and styles of the crocus flower. An expensive spice with a rich colour, texture and aroma, it has a whole host of health benefits, including elevating mood, which is why it is known as the 'sunshine spice'. Studies show that saffron reduces the severity of the symptoms of premenstrual syndrome (PMS), mild to moderate depression and Alzheimer's. Additionally, saffron is good for the skin, for digestion, circulation and the nervous system. Saffron appears as an important medicinal herb in many ancient texts, including those belonging to Ayurveda, Unani,* and Chinese medicine.

---

* 'Unaani' means 'Greek' and Unani medicine is an ancient Greek system of medicine based on the qualities of four temperaments and four humours. The Unani system of medicine was introduced in India by Arabs and Persians around the eleventh century. Today, India is one of the leading countries in the practice of Unani medicine.

Tips on how to use saffron

According to my grandmother and my mother, you're not meant to consume saffron strands raw; they should always be roasted. This should be done in a hot pan, after which the strands can be crumbled by hand and stored in a small airtight jar for future use. There is a technique to doing this properly so that the saffron strands don't burn. This not only brings out the flavour but is considered to be better for health. Always be careful to handle the saffron with a dry spoon or dry fingers – be careful never to wet the strands. Here's our family technique:

1. Heat a pan for 1 minute until hot. Add the saffron strands, taking care not to burn them. They should turn a deeper red but not brown colour.

2. Remove from the heat and spread out the saffron strands.

3. Leave them for 1–2 minutes until you're able to crumble the strands between your fingers and make something like a saffron dust.

4. Put this dust into an airtight container or jar.

Pigments of the spice have been found in 50,000-year-old paintings in Iran. Alexander the Great supposedly bathed in warm water sprinkled with saffron to heal his wounds after battle. He and his men also ate saffron rice and drank saffron tea to rejuvenate their strength.

Star anise is a star-shaped rust- or wood-coloured spice. It is the dried fruit of an Asian evergreen tree, *Illicium verum*, and has many culinary and medicinal uses. It has a liquorice and aniseed flavour and is naturally sweet and very aromatic. It can boost the immune system, protect against respiratory infections by reducing inflammation, is a great remedy for colds and can aid relaxation and sleep. Star anise can be simmered whole when making chai, but you can also get it in powder form, called Badian powder, and add it to your spice blends or bakes that way.

Turmeric is one of the most powerful medicinal spices and is anti-inflammatory, packed with antioxidants and has anti-cancerous properties. It helps detoxify the liver, cure colds and flus, stimulates digestion, boosts immunity and enhances the complexion. Turmeric is made from the rhizome of the plant *Cucurma longa*, another member of the ginger family. It gives a curry its yellow colour and is the spice we turn to when we're feeling under the weather, both as prevention and cure for colds and flu. An important healing agent in Ayurveda, turmeric's active component is curcumin, which is an antioxidant and anti-inflammatory and helps with degenerative diseases, such as arthritis, as well as helping to lower bad cholesterol and boost general immunity. Ayurveda recognises turmeric as a heating spice, contributing bitter, pungent and astringent tastes.

Sweeteners

Sweetness is key to traditional chai and most Indians prefer their chai 'extra sweet', drinking a small cup with an intense concentration of spices, sweetness and strength.

Sugar is most commonly used in making chai, but the healthier and – in my opinion tastier – option is mineral-rich jaggery. Known as 'gur' in India, where more than 70 per cent of its production takes place, jaggery is a type of unrefined sugar, prepared without the separation of molasses and crystals. It is sold in large golden to dark brown blocks, which are broken into smaller pieces.

After the juice is extracted from fresh sugarcane, it is filtered and boiled in large iron pans and stirred continuously. Soda or bhindi (okra) juice is then added, and the brownish foam that floats to the top is removed to get the distinctive golden colour. Once the juice has thickened, it is poured into block-shaped moulds to cool. Jaggery can also be made with date palm, which is popular in parts of East and South India as well as in Myanmar.

Ayurvedic practitioners have been using jaggery for thousands of years. It is considered high in various minerals and vitamins, from magnesium and potassium to iron and B complex. Jaggery contains longer chains of sucrose, which means it takes longer for the body to digest, releasing energy more slowly than refined sugar. The magnesium in jaggery is said to also boost nervous system function, and its high iron content could potentially protect against anaemia.

There's a delicious earthy sweetness to jaggery that adds depth of flavour to the chai. You can, of course, use alternative sweeteners such as stevia or honey. Or, if you're able to enjoy chai without any sweetening, even better! Some may say this takes a lot away from the flavour, but to me it's rather like having sugar in any other hot drink: a matter of preference or something you become accustomed to.

Chai story: My great-grandmother's heirlooms

LONDON, 2021

It's summer in London, the year after Covid hit us. I'm sitting in the garden with my grandmother, whom I call Bhabhi, sipping *masala chai on a glorious summer's day.*

---

* The names of people in my grandparents' generation (and indeed further back) were very long, and so many of them were known by shortened versions or even entirely different names. While my grandmother's given name is Bhanumati, she was known as Bhabhi, a name that is a respectful reference to a brother's wife, probably because my grandfather had so many brothers and sisters. My grandfather's name is Prabudhas, which became Babubhai ('bhai' is an addition to the name of any uncle or elder used to denote respect) and eventually simply Babhai. My maternal grandfather, Laljiseth-bhai, was known as Bapuji, and my maternal grandmother, Lakshmiben, was Baa. My mother's aunt was known by everyone as Faiba, which, in the same way as Bhabhi, refers to a father's sister, so means 'aunt'. These names, used by everyone in the family, became part of the individual's character and identity.

She is telling me about her earliest memories of drinking chai. She was eight years old, most likely, and one of her uncles or 'mama'* made chai every day for her and her nani, her maternal grandmother. This was her family unit. Bhabhi grew up in Sarvar, a small lakeside village in Gujarat, taking her maternal grandmother, her nani, to be her mother and living with her three mamas. She remembers every detail of her childhood in this village as though it were yesterday. The day would always start with rotlo (thick millet flour rotis), spread with home-made makhand (clarified butter), after which they would drink chai, always from a glass rakabi (a deep saucer) from which they would, as is custom, slurp the hot drink.

Everything they ate and drank from the makhand on the rotlo, the chai, the dahi (yoghurt) they had with their meals, the chaas (buttermilk or lassi) they drank to cool their bodies and the ghee used for cooking, was made with the milk from their own cows. The cow is worshipped in India – in gratitude for all that the animal provides. And it's not just dairy products they provide. Cow dung, called 'gobar' or 'chaan', has been and is still used extensively for fuel throughout the country – Bhabhi remembers using only cow dung with wood to cook rotlas, among other things. Cows were also used for ploughing fields and for transportation. And lastly, cow-dung patties are put together to make the walls and floors of village homes. Since cow dung is a very poor conductor of moisture and heat, it creates balanced interior temperatures in winter and summer: warm in winter and cool in the summer. As well as being associated with deities like Krishna and thus having religious significance, this is why

---

* In Gujarati and Hindi, there are different names for each family member, so your mum's brother is a mama, while your dad's brother is kaka, and some of these names also vary from Gujarati to Hindi.

the cow is called *Gaay mata*, '*gaay*' meaning 'cow' and '*mata*' 'mother'.

Bhabhi vividly remembers the cows and buffalos standing outside her grandmother's house. She was too scared to milk them herself as they weren't used to her hands, so her grandmother would always do this. And since their own cows didn't produce enough for their own use, she would often go and get more from the village cows.

And so Bhabhi grew up in this peaceful village in Gujarat while her siblings grew up with their parents in the coastal town of Mombasa in Kenya. When she was born in 1934, her own mother, Baa, had left her in her home village with Bhabhi's nani, my great-great-grandmother, and travelled back in a ship to Mombasa. This was a month-long journey and so, taking her three young sons, she must have decided to leave behind her newly born daughter for practicality. Bhabhi's father had moved to the port town of Mombasa years before, just after his marriage, as part of a migratory wave of Indian traders, most of whom were recruited by the British from north-west India to build the region's railways (1890s–1900), though my great-grandfather was one of the many voluntary migrants who decided to join the settlers who stayed on in East Africa after building the railways. Many of these migrants like him came from Gujarat and, to a lesser extent, Punjab and Goa, including various castes of Hindus, Muslims, Sikhs and Parsees.

I've spent many childhood holidays in Mombasa as my grandmother's brother and his children still live there, as did Baa, my grandmother's mother, until she passed away some twenty years ago, and while my grandmother was married in Uganda, she gave birth to my father in Mombasa. I still remember sitting with Baa on the swing in her Mombasa home, which we took to be our Mombasa home, spending so many holidays there, eating 'chusni *keri', the juiciest of juicy mangos, and watching television with her. More than chai, though, I remember her making 'haar' or garlands of beautiful white frangipanis with my grandmother for the deities in the temple, using a large needle and thick thread to piece together the flowers in the morning. The back doors would be fully open, letting in a very calm and warm morning breeze. And in the evening, when the breeze was slightly cooler, she and my grandmother would be sitting together on the sofa watching* The Bold and the Beautiful, *and even though neither of them understood English, somehow they knew exactly what went on. I can still picture them glued to the television, eating popcorn, which they both devoured, and which my grandmother makes fresh even to this day a few times a week.*

Writing this book now, I wish I could ask her the questions I'm asking my grandmother, like how she felt leaving her daughter in Sarvar with her mother for so many years, and whether she liked Mombasa, though it seems with their generation, as with my own parents' generation, that they just got on with life, made the best of the situation they were in, and when I ask about how they felt doing something, it's almost like the first time they've thought about how they actually felt.

For Bhabhi, her childhood in this small village turned out to be her most blissful days, which she still tells me about today. She describes her childhood spent as the princess of this village – and she was certainly treated like a princess by Nani. Her day started by drawing water from the kuvo (well), before attending school for a couple of hours, usually 10 a.m. until midday. Some days she would carry crockery down to the lake for washing, and then fetch grass for their cows and buffalos. She made her way to their fields, by a shortcut that meant wading through water, so that she could help weed them in order for the grains to grow – in the village they grew their own baajro (millet), jowar (sorghum),

matth (mat beans), mung beans and urad daal (black gram).
She explained the process of threshing the grains in August or
September, how the edible part was loosened from the scaly chaff
that surrounds it. This ancient method involved spreading out
the harvest in a field just outside the village, tying the cows and
buffalos together, five to seven of them, and letting them walk over
the grains in a circle until the different parts separated.

Years later, when her father finally came to take her to
Mombasa (after a failed first attempt by Baa to collect her when
she was nine, when Bhabhi simply refused to believe Baa was
her mother and was adamant she wanted to stay in India), the
entire village came to say goodbye. When I visited Sarvar as a
teenager with my brother, I remember how everyone's face would
light up when we mentioned my grandmother – she was certainly
popular. And when she finally left with her father, who she was
meeting for the first time, they had just reached Mumbai when
her mum's brothers, who she had lived with, came to Mumbai
to gift her silver janjri, to remind her of her nani, as she had no
idea when she would see Bhabhi again. (She did go back many
years later with my grandfather and her three young boys while
her nani was still alive (see page 122)). Each year, my grand-
mother would wear the janjri at Navratri, the nine-day dance
festival celebrating the nine forms of Goddess Durga, she tells me;
and when I got married at twenty-five, she gifted these janjri to
me. She still checks that I've worn them at Navratri and family
weddings.

---

* Janjri are heavy ankle bells that make a beautiful sound when a woman
walks. While they are fashionable, they also serve a purpose, activating the
lymph glands and boosting immunity. Nowadays, we usually only wear
them on special occasions, such as Navratri or at a wedding dance or garba
(Gujarati dance) event.

Bhabhi remembers her nani having chai in the morning and in the afternoon after waking up from a short nap, something my grandmother has also always done. The afternoon chai was simply boiled milk, water and tea leaves, usually with no extra spices, although Bhabhi remembers her grating ginger into the pot now and then, and she would often make more, offering chai to the women who passed by their home holding pots on their heads and by their hips on their way to fetch water. As my grandmother reminisces about these cups of chai that shaped her day, I reflect on how the history of chai interweaves with that of my own family, how chai has been a constant, the way my father still loves to grate ginger when making his own chai, the small jar of chai masala my mother always carries on her travels, and that I now sell chai spices as my business. The chronology of when chai became popular in India, how it filtered through from cities to villages and when spices started being used might be nebulous, but it was clearly very much a part of daily life by the 1930s, even in the smallest of villages, and as far away as Mombasa and Uganda, where both sets of my great-grandparents made chai daily.

CHAI
RECIPES

How you drink your chai depends on the spices you prefer, and how sweet and milky you like it. Equally, it could vary depending on mood, season and time of day. On a cold winter's day, for example, you might want a very gingery chai for extra warmth, or even a sweet and soothing chocolate chai. If you're recovering from a cold, perhaps a Kashmiri kawha, which comes from the beautiful Himalayan Vale of Kashmir, or a warming spicy kadha? When you're feeling sleepy, an extra-strong or 'kadak' chai might be needed as a pick-me-up, or perhaps a South Indian-style filter coffee. And if you need a nightcap, you might want to sip a turmeric chai with some saffron strands and nutmeg to help your mind to relax. Each spice has its own array of benefits for the body and mind, they are anti-inflammatory and aid digestion, and each one adds a different flavour to your cup of chai.

This chapter focuses on chai and spice-infused drink recipes from across India, as well as some of my own creations, including Chocolate Ginger Chai, Rose Chai, my own version of Turmeric Chai, and Pumpkin Chai Latte. I've also included a selection of other Indian-spiced drinks, including both savoury and sweet lassis.

The proportion of water to milk in all the chai recipes is done according to the consistency of the milk you are using. If you're using full-fat dairy milk, you can use a higher water to milk ratio. Semi-skimmed dairy milk and most plant-based milks, including oat milk and soya milk, work best with a half-and-half mix. However, if you're using a light almond milk, you may need to use more milk and less water. Check whether your plant-based milk is sweetened too, in which case you may want to add less sugar or jaggery.

Jaggery or sugar can be used interchangeably in these recipes, although, as I've said, I prefer the flavour of jaggery. If you'd like to try an alternative, coconut sugar is similar in flavour to jaggery, and is made from coconut palm sap. You could also use maple syrup if you like its taste; and if you are avoiding sugar, then stevia makes for a healthy, all-natural substitute for sugar and is considered more natural than other artificial sweeteners. While honey can also be used to sweeten drinks, it should never be heated or be added to hot drinks, according to Ayurveda. Heated honey in any form can lead to 'ama', or toxicity in the body.

Equipment

To make a cup of chai the Indian way, the first step is to boil the tea leaves with the water and milk in a pan rather than making it in a kettle. It may also be useful to have the following equipment:

Pan: a small saucepan to heat the chai brew.

Strainer: you will ideally be using loose tea rather than teabags to make a cup of chai and therefore will need a small strainer so that you can strain the liquid and have a cup of chai without the tea leaves coming into your mouth.

Grater: if using fresh ginger, something we use at home almost daily, the best way to ensure you extract the juice and flavour well is to grate it using a stainless-steel hand-held food grater.

Peeler/spoon: this is used to peel fresh ginger (you can easily peel ginger skin by pressing the edge of a spoon against the skin and scraping it). If you're cooking with ginger, you'll always need to remove the skin. However, if you're using it in tea you will most likely be pouring the chai through a strainer, so it is not necessary to remove the skin; just make sure you wash the ginger well.

Pestle and mortar: if using whole spices, a pestle and mortar is useful to crush the spices before boiling them with your chai. The pounding of spices like whole cardamoms, cloves, peppercorns and cinnamon sticks will help extract the flavour from them and give much more zest and aroma to the chai. If using powdered spices or a powdered spice blend, you won't need a pestle and mortar.

Pan or wok: a small heavy-bottomed pan or wok is useful if dry-roasting the spices, again to bring out their flavour.

High-speed blender: a strong blender is useful for various drinks, lassis and smoothies, and enables the blending of dates, nuts and more.

For the rest of the recipes, I'm assuming you have a conventional oven and a well-equipped kitchen and can adapt the recipes to what you have.

A note on milk and measurements: unless stated otherwise, you can use any type of milk you like to make these recipes. 1 cup = 250ml approx.

Spice Blends

Most Indian families have their own distinctive spice blend, which they prepare in advance in quantity and use whenever they want to make a cup of chai. Spice blends are convenient, avoiding the need to grind or crush spices each time chai is made. They are also portable, allowing people to carry their chai blend with them to work or on trips, boiling it with milk and water or simply stirring it into a cup of plain tea. Here I will give my mum's spice-blend recipe, which comprises grated ginger, crushed cardamoms, cinnamon, black pepper, white pepper, nutmeg and cloves. You can make any tweaks you like to this mixture to adjust the flavour to your taste. For example, if you want to reduce the spiciness, you could use a little less pepper, or no white pepper at all.

My Mum's Spice Blend

3 teaspoons ground ginger
2 teaspoons ground cardamom
1½ teaspoons ground cinnamon
1½ teaspoons ground black pepper
¼ teaspoon ground nutmeg
pinch of ground clove (optional)

Mix together all the ingredients and store in an airtight container or a sprinkling jar to use daily, when needed. This masala mix will last you for around three weeks if you're drinking chai every day. To keep the spice mix tasting its best, store your container out of direct sunlight, for up to three months.

To make chai with this spice mix, boil together:

½ cup milk
½ cup water
1–2 teaspoons tea leaves
1 teaspoon jaggery or sugar
¼–½ teaspoon chai spice mix

Pour through a strainer into a cup and enjoy.

You can also carry this spice mix with you when travelling and simply add this into your teacup or mug when making a cup of tea using a teabag. Put the spice mix at the bottom of the cup with the teabag, than add the boiling water slowly on top, stirring as you pour, so that all the spices get mixed into the hot water.

Chai story: By the Hanuman temple

MAHUVA, GUJARAT

Two hours away from the city of Bhavnagar in Gujarat is the pil-grimage centre of Chiktrakoot, the home and ashram of renowned spiritual leader Morari Bapu. Since I was a teenager, on most of my visits to India, I either travel to Bapu's hometown of Mahuva to see him or centre my India travels around a katha, a nine-day Ramayana recital he would be doing somewhere in the country. And so, on one of these visits to Mahuva, in my twenties, a small crowd of us are sitting by Bapu in front of the golden statue of the

monkey god, Hanuman (or Hanumanji, as we call him – the *'ji'* being a respectful suffix). *The flickering rays of sunlight that were until now pouring through the canopy of leaves above us fade away as the sky deepens in colour and evening approaches. This is Bapu's place of meeting, morning and evening, rather like his office, where he reads the papers, meets anyone who has come from nearby villages, towns and cities across India and indeed from different parts of the world, where one of the followers might sing or ask him a question, and sometimes Bapu shares wisdom as he sways breezily on his hindoro, a type of seated swing.*

There are around thirty of us this evening and the smell of sweet chai wafts our way, overpowering every other scent. I hear movement behind me; cups are being passed around. No sooner have I been given one than a man appears with a matt silver pot and pours the fragrant brew from the spout, steam escaping into the warm air.

Chai here is always extra sweet, as is mostly the way in Gujarat, and this is how Bapu likes it. This is why chai goes hand-in-hand with ganthia (savoury crackers), thepla (spiced rotis, almost synonymous with being Gujarati) or poha (a breakfast dish made with flattened rice, stir fried with onions, spices and small potato cubes) (see page 230), something I grew up eating a couple of times a month on a weekend morning and which my mum still makes so perfectly today. Chai also needs to be kadak (strong) in its tea infusion, and boiled properly, so that the colour deepens and becomes a darker, albeit milky, brown.

Soon it is dusk, the moon starts to brighten in the sky and the evening aarti (devotional song of praise sung to the deities) begins. The sounds of a conch summons us to silence and an air of calm spreads through Chiktrakoot. The priest who looks after this temple walks towards the larger-than-life statue of Hanumanji, towering ahead of us and glowing in the evening light. The priest stands there as he does the ritualistic aarti, his head reaching the deity's navel. In his left hand he holds a ghanta, a brass puja (prayer) bell, its echoing sound filling the open space, loud yet meditative; in his right hand he is swinging a metallic bowl filled with coals and dhoop (incense), smoke swiftly escaping into the air, creating circles as he moves it in large circular clockwise motions, swiftly dispersing and filling the space in front of Hanumanji. This is a daily ritual, here and in large and small temples all over India, as well as in homes and on the banks of the Ganges, but there's something ceremoniously soul-soothing, healing and beautiful about it, each and every time.

At first, he stands facing Hanumanji, with his back to us, and then he turns to his right and does a few rounds, then towards us, and finally to his right, expressing gratitude to the gods all around, and purifying and cleansing the air. He bends down in front of Hanumanji as he does the aarti to the small Ganesh statue sitting at the monkey god's feet. Ganesh is the god of luck, and the remover of obstacles.

The priest is singing quietly, but all that reaches our ears is the beautiful trance-like sound of the bell. Bapu looks ahead at the golden statue as the aarti finishes and I take a deep breath and close my eyes, taking a snapshot of the extraordinary peace that reverberates through the space.

The aarti ends, the ringing stops and the priest places the dhoop by Hanumanji's feet for a few moments, smoke escaping into the air, spreading over the golden deity. And then, as he brings it back towards us, the musky fragrance of the dhoop floats through the atmosphere, the smell of camphor woody, floral, menthol-like, reminding me of the church services of my childhood days. He takes it to Bapu first, who, as is custom, moves his hands as a gesture to take the smoke and waft it over his head, after which the priest offers it around and we all follow suit.

Sometimes, Bapu continues to talk after this, or listens to the people surrounding him – there may even be music, some shaayari (spoken poetry) – but today he decides to leave, after responding to a few questions. As he stands up, everyone around him stands; some people move towards his car if they want to speak to him, make eye contact, others move ahead so they can wave as his car leaves. He stands by the short gate that separates his swing from the crowd to speak to someone quietly then looks around and smiles as he leaves.

Another day with Bapu comes to an end.

Chai with Spices

Adrak Chai

While masala chai can be made with all the spices, it can also be made with a single spice, most commonly ginger or cardamom. So, here's a spicy adrak (ginger) chai recipe, boiled with the crushed or grated root, warming and healing, great for the colder months and full of antioxidants. Ginger has a whole host of health benefits, from helping ease nausea to lowering blood pressure and aiding digestion. When boiled with cow's milk, ginger can sometimes curdle the milk, so avoid this by heating the ingredients together without the milk and then adding the milk at the end of the process.

Makes 2 cups

1cm/½ inch piece of fresh ginger
1½ cup water
2–3 teaspoons loose tea leaves
1 cup milk
2 tablespoons sugar

Wash and crush or grate the ginger, to allow the juice to easily seep into the water (you don't need to peel the ginger as you will be pouring the chai through a strainer, but you can peel it if you like – see page 77). Pour the water into the tea pan and add the crushed or grated ginger and tea leaves. Bring to the boil and let this simmer on a medium heat. After 1–2 minutes, add the milk and sugar and boil until it has that rich brown tea colour. Strain into cups while piping hot.

Elaichi Chai

This is chai boiled with aromatic crushed elaichi (cardamom), less spicy than ginger, but with warming floral notes. Cardamom and ginger are the most prominent spices used in chai, over and above all the other chai spices. Cardamom has numerous health benefits, from aiding digestion and freshening the breath to helping lower blood pressure. It is also rich in antioxidants.

Crushing the pods before adding them to your brew allows for the flavour to release and infuse into the chai properly. You could use a pestle and mortar to do this, or crush the pods on a chopping board with something heavy.

Makes 2 cups

1½ cups water
3 green cardamom pods, crushed or opened
2–3 teaspoons loose tea leaves
1 cup milk
1 tablespoon jaggery or sugar

Pour the water into the tea pan and add the crushed cardamom pods and tea leaves. Bring to the boil and let this simmer on a medium heat. After 1–2 minutes, add milk and sugar and boil until it has that rich brown tea colour. Strain into cups while piping hot.

Saunf Chai

Adding saunf (fennel) seeds to chai gives a wonderful anise flavour. Fennel is great for reducing digestive discomfort and also has cooling properties, bringing down any internal heat in the body, thereby helping issues like acne.

Makes 2 cups

¼ teaspoon cardamom powder
    or 2 crushed cardamom pods
1 teaspoon fennel seeds
1½ cups water
2–3 teaspoons tea leaves
1 tablespoon jaggery or sugar
1 cup milk

If using cardamom pods, crush them along with the fennel seeds and cardamom pods slightly in a pestle and mortar. If using cardamom powder, you don't need to crush the fennel seeds as the flavour will still be strong, so this is optional.

Boil all the ingredients except the milk for a few minutes on a low to medium heat, then add the milk and boil for a little longer. Once boiled, switch to a high heat, let the tea rise to the top and reduce the heat. Do this a couple of times before straining the tea into your cup.

Kesar Chai

Kesar (saffron) is a delicious and luxurious addition to your morning or anytime cup of tea. Boiling the chai with saffron adds a golden hue to the brew, and the spice is also calming, so helps with any stress or anxiety, and is high in antioxidants. I quite like adding cardamom to this, as the two spices complement each other, but you could also make it with saffron alone.

Makes 1 cup

½ cups water
½ cup milk
pinch/few saffron strands
¼ teaspoon or less cardamom powder,
    or 1 cardamom pod, crushed
1 teaspoon tea leaves
1 teaspoon sugar (optional)

Combine the water and milk in a pan. Add the saffron, cardamom and loose tea. Add sugar if using. Bring to the boil and then reduce the heat, then bring it back to the boil a few times. Pour through a sieve into a cup.

Chai with Herbs and Leaves

Leeli Chai

'Leeli' means green, and leeli chai is the name given to lemongrass chai in India. Lemongrass is a green-coloured tall grass that grows as a shrub. I've had chai boiled with lemongrass on the streets of Mumbai and in Gujarat, sometimes with just lemongrass but sometimes with additional spices. It has a fresh, earthy and herbal flavour, which I love, and feels calming and restorative. It's also high in antioxidants, potassium and vitamin C and is good for digestion.

Makes 2 cups

1½ cup water
1 lemongrass stalk, cut into 1 inch/2.5cm pieces,
    or 1 tablespoon dried lemongrass
2–3 teaspoon tea leaves
½ teaspoon chai masala mix (optional) (see page 79)
1 tablespoon jaggery or sugar
1 cup milk

Simmer all the ingredients except the milk on a low to medium heat until the brew is a darker shade of brown, then add the milk and let it all boil for a few more minutes. Switch to a high heat, let the tea rise to the top and then reduce the heat. Do this a couple more times before straining the mix into your cup. To make the chai more potent and spicy, you can add some chai masala mix or grate in some fresh ginger.

Tulsi Chai

Also called holy basil, the tulsi plant is one of the most revered plants in India. Boiling chai with tulsi leaves gives it a distinctive herbal aroma and is calming and elevating. Holy basil has adaptogenic properties, meaning it helps the body adapt to stress.

Makes 2 cups

10–12 tulsi leaves
1½ cups water
2–3 teaspoons tea leaves
small piece ginger, grated (optional)
1 tablespoon jaggery or sugar
1 cup milk

You can crush the tulsi leaves slightly in a mortar and pestle, as this will bring out the flavour, but this is optional. Put all the ingredients except for the milk into your pan, bring to the boil and simmer for a few minutes on a low to medium heat, then add the milk and let this boil for a little longer. Once boiled, switch to a high heat, let the tea rise to the top and reduce the heat. Repeat this a couple of times before straining the tea into your cup.

Pudina Chai

This is a fragrant and refreshing chai made with pudina (mint). If you love peppermint tea, you'll most likely love this chai. You can give it a spice kick by adding grated ginger or any other spices, but the flavour of the mint will come through much stronger if using it alone. Mint can soothe bloating and help digestion, relieve headaches, has anti-bacterial properties and boosts the immune system.

Makes 2 cups

8–12 fresh mint leaves
1½ cups water
2–3 teaspoons tea leaves
1 tablespoon jaggery or sugar
1 cup milk

Crush the mint leaves lightly using a pestle and mortar if you can, to allow the flavours to release into the brew. Boil the mint leaves in the water until the colour of the water is green, then add the tea leaves and jaggery or sugar. Now add the milk and let this simmer for a few more minutes. Switch to a high heat, let the tea rise to the top and reduce the heat. Do this a couple of times before straining the tea into your cup.

Tejpatta Chai

Indian bay leaves, known as 'tejpatta', are found in the tropical Himalayas, Nilgiri hills, Khasi hills and Sikkim. You will usually find them in their dry form. They have a distinct fragrance and have a sweet cinnamon-like taste. Bay leaves are anti-inflammatory, antifungal and antibacterial, they aid digestion, help to regulate blood-sugar levels and cholesterol levels and lower inflammation.

Makes 2 cups

1–2 bay leaves
1½ cups water
2–3 teaspoons tea leaves (depending on how strong you
    like your tea)
1 tablespoon jaggery or sugar
1 cup milk

Boil the bay leaves in the water until the colour of the water is green, then add the tea leaves and jaggery or sugar. Now add the milk and let this boil for a few minutes. Once boiled, switch to a high heat, let the tea rise to the top and reduce the heat. Do this a couple of times before straining into your cup.

Kari Patta Chai

Kari patta (curry leaves) are generally used in curries and daals. They're added to the tadka curry base with other spices, before the curry or daal itself is made. However, you can also make chai with curry leaves, though it is less common. The curry leaf is glossy and has a strong aroma. The antioxidants and proteins in curry leaves are said to strengthen hair, so they are often added to hair oils. They are also rich in vitamin A and thus beneficial to the eyes, and they help reduce stress and can lower blood-sugar levels too.

Makes 2 cups

3–4 curry leaves
1½ cups water
2–3 teaspoons tea leaves (depending on how strong you like your tea)
1 tablespoon jaggery or sugar
1 cup milk

Boil the curry leaves in the water until the colour of the water is green, then add the tea leaves and jaggery or sugar. Now add the milk and let this boil for a little longer. Once boiled, switch to a high heat, let the tea rise to the top and reduce the heat. Do this a couple of times before straining into your cup.

Chai story: Baa's gor keri

A few weeks every summer would always be spent with my mum's family in Loughborough, a town in the Leicestershire country-side. My mum settled here with her family as immigrants, after the president of Uganda, Idi Amin, ordered the expulsion of his country's Indian minority in 1972, giving them ninety days to leave the country. While my father's family settled in London, my mother's family created their home in Loughborough. My grandparents' home in Loughborough was a second home for us, which we escaped to during the holidays, enjoying a slower pace of life in the English countryside and spending time with my mum's parents, our younger cousins and my uncle, who I called Dilip mama, and who would take us for walks in ancient woodlands known as The Outwoods.*

---

* As with all other relations, we have different names for uncles and aunts on the father's side and on the mother's side. A mum's brother is called mama, so for me it is Dilip mama (Dilip is his name).

I remember my mum's father, whom I called Bapuji, doing headstands every morning in his off-white cotton trousers or 'home pyjamas', his full-white head of hair resting on a pillow for ten minutes. Meanwhile, Baa (my maternal grandmother) and Faiba, my grandfather's sister, who lived with them, would be completing their puja (morning prayers) upstairs and when they came down soon after, we would all sit down together for breakfast. Bapuji, apparently, deemed it unhealthy to overboil milk – Indians like to double or triple boil chai – so he would opt for English tea, with masala spices stirred in, which he would sip with toast or taadhi rotli (cold roti from the previous evening), usually after a bowl of Weetabix served with warm milk. These memories date from after Baa and Bapuji retired – before this, they both worked in a factory nearby that manufactured shoe-laces, getting a daily long walk on the way to and from work.

On holiday weekends or whenever they had guests staying, Baa and Faiba would be in the kitchen, cooking up a feast. They were lifelong companions. Ever since Faiba's husband passed away early in life, they had lived together, in the hills of Kabale in Uganda for many years, and now in the UK. Faiba was a very gentle lady with all-white hair and an even softer voice. When I was a little older, a teenager, I would often massage her legs in the evening when I was visiting.

If there were more of us staying for a weekend, my dad and perhaps my kaka (my uncle, Dad's brother) visiting from London – both families were and still are very close – or other family and close friends visiting from Leicester, Baa, with the help of Faiba and, when my uncle got married, with the help of my aunt Urvashi mami, would swiftly cook up a breakfast spread of various fresh Gujarati delights. There might be fried puris and potato curry, or thepla (spiced rotis), sometimes bhakri, a thicker and more filling version of a roti served with athanu (pickles) *such as Baa's delicious gor keri, a tangy jaggery-sweetened pickle – or even a saani (plate) of fresh, steaming dhokla, everyone's favourite yellow, soft, cake-like savoury snack, usually served with green chutney (you can find the recipe for this in my cookbook, Saffron Soul) – all served with garam chai, of course. Rather like us, the Gujaratis in north-west London, they too had a whole East African Gujarati community in Leicester, with a smaller community in Loughborough.*

Baa made jars of gor keri, a raw mango pickle, sweetened with jaggery, for any guests and family who visited, including our family – she would send a large jar back with my mother after our visits to last months for us all, including my paternal grandparents, uncles and aunts. The making of this was quite a process (there's a recipe on page 266 that is the simplified version we make in my family now). Baa would first warm a large amount of oil, in which she would slowly melt the jaggery. Then, removing it from the heat, she would stir in lots of lime juice. In another pan, she would again heat a little oil, add roasted and coarsely ground coriander seeds, rai na kuriya (split yellow mustard seeds), akha mari (whole peppercorns), some cinnamon sticks and a few tablespoons of fennel seeds. Once this was cooked, she would add this to the oil and jaggery mixture, which would have cooled a little by now but would still have a runny consistency. This pan would be left in the cool garage, covered with a funiko (a metallic plate,*

---

* There were many Swahili words like 'funiko' that the Ugandan Gujaratis adopted and which we grew up using as part of our Gujarati sentences, thinking they were Gujarati words. It was only in my Gujarati language classes that we all took as a GCSE that I realised I was using the Swahili word for things like 'dizzi' – banana ('kela' in Gujarati), or 'kisu' – knife ('chaku' in Gujarati) and 'paasi' – ironing ('istri' in Gujarati). These little anecdotes from language to food (using root vegetables like cassava and plantain only found in Africa to make curry and other Indian dishes which we eat at home to this day) weave together the story of migration and integration.

like a lid) and stirred a few times a day for a week to ensure the oil and jaggery didn't start separating – the jaggery, which becomes solid at room temperature, would start sinking to the bottom, and so stirring it regularly would ensure it remained a mixture. Baa, Faiba or my mother would go to the garage to stir the mixture around three times a day. In Uganda, raw mangos, slightly sour and green, were easily available, so Baa would chop these, along with carrots and kharek (dried dates), into small pieces, boil them for a few minutes and then leave them to dry in the sun for a few days, afterwards stirring them into the jaggery and oil mixture too. While a key ingredient in this pickle is the raw mango (the name itself is a combination of the words 'gor', meaning 'jaggery', and 'keri', meaning 'mango'), they realised that this delicious pickle can be made without the raw mango if it's not available. In Uganda, they made it with cassava.

Back at the breakfast banquet, there would always be large jars of nashta, crunchy fried savoury snacks like ganthia (popular crispy Gujarati snacks made from chickpea flour), sev mamra (a puffed rice and chickpea noodle snack) and farsi puri (a crispy deep-fried Indian bread – the word 'farsi' meaning 'crispy' and 'flaky'), which they would make every couple of months, a half-day process during which they would make several varieties. It is now very easy to find these snacks in Indian and Gujarati shops in places like Wembley, Tooting and Leicester, where the Indian roads feel like a mini India, with temples, restaurants, jewellery shops, paan (betel-nut leaf with sweet fillings eaten after a meal) shops, and vegetable shops selling all the Indian vegetables we use in curries, such as karela (bitter gourd), dudhi (bottle gourd), bhindi (okra), valor (field beans), tindora (ivy gourd) and more.

Bapuji was strict about fried foods and would tell Baa and Faiba not to indulge in or even make these savoury snacks, but he still had a few here and there – they're too delicious to resist. He certainly had some impact on my uncle Dilip mama, who, since Bapuji's passing, became an avid marathon runner year on year and around the world. He is running the Marathon des Sables as I write this, the ultramarathon across the Sahara Desert. My mum, too, has done many a bike ride around the world, from Vietnam, Rajasthan and Kenya, to trekking in Macchu Picchu, Kilimanjaro, and this year Everest Base Camp. I'm sure Bapuji would be looking on with pride – and words of caution!

Over the years, we visited Loughborough less often – I wish I had visited more. My mum effectively had three parents, Baa, Bapuji and Faiba, and the last of them, Baa, passed away in 2022, at the age of ninety-six. There's lots of food I wish I'd learned how to make from her, from the sweet gor thepla (roti sweetened with jaggery) she made so well, to her gor keri. I wish I'd asked her how she used to make her chai masala in a grinder, what proportions of spices she used, how long she would roast them in the oven, her techniques all perfected before the days of buying ground spices and mixing them together quickly and easily. If there's one thing I learned from her, it was the attitude of abundance, feeding each and every guest with no sense of anything lacking, even though she worked in factories and had a small house; of doing things very quickly with zero fuss and making everything she did look totally effortless. There was never any compromise with food and variety, there was warmth and invitation, and there was always chai!

Other Flavours and Regional Chais

Rose Chai

Adding rose syrup to chai is something truly divine, lending soothing floral notes to the classic masala flavour and giving the tea a pretty pink colour. We used to serve this as a special in my café. You can use any rose syrup, but the traditional Indian rose syrup is certainly unique, richer and thicker, and is available in most Indian stores and online. It also gives the drink that wonderful pink colour. Another option is to add rose water, which gives a lovely, gentle rose flavour, and all the health benefits that come with rose without the syrupy sweetness. Rose is a great anti-inflammatory – it calms the skin when used topically. The *Rosa damascena* plant, called 'the flower of Prophet Mohammad' by Iranians, was traditionally used for the treatment of abdominal and chest pains, strengthening the heart and helping with menstrual bleeding, digestive problems and constipation.* It is also rich in antioxidants, helping to keep us youthful. Since rose and cardamom complement each other very well, cardamom is the second spice used in this chai. A few saffron strands are optional, but will add richness and an extra mood-boosting effect.

---

* *Science Direct* https://www.sciencedirect.com/science/article/pii/ S2225411015000954

Makes 1 cup

1 cup water
1 teaspoon rose syrup or rose water
½ teaspoon cardamom powder
    (or 3 cardamom pods, open and crushed a little)
pinch of saffron strands (optional)
1 teaspoon tea leaves
2 teaspoons brown sugar
    (NB if you are using rose syrup, omit the sugar)
sprinkle of dried rose petals (optional)
½ cup milk

Boil all the ingredients except the milk for a few minutes on a low to medium heat, then add the milk and let this boil for a little longer. Once boiled, switch to a high heat, let the tea rise to the top and reduce the heat. Do this a couple of times before straining into your cup.

Irani Chai

Irani chai was first introduced in India by Persian immigrants who arrived in the mid-1700s. They migrated from Mumbai east to Pune and finally to Hyderabad, which explains why Irani Chai is also known as Hyderabadi Dum Chai, the word 'dum' meaning to slowly brew the tea on a low flame and cover it with a lid to lock in the aroma. Traditionally this sweet, creamy chai is made by slowly brewing spices and black tea together with a type of milk solid called mawa or khoya, made by simmering full-fat milk for hours until the liquid evaporates and the pale yellow solids remain. The tea and milk mixtures are prepared separately, and the creamy milk mixture poured on top of the brewed tea. Nowadays many use condensed milk or cream instead of khoya, which simplifies the process.

You'll find Irani Chai in the famous Irani cafés of Mumbai, Pune and Hyderabad. These appeared in the 1920s and were an important cultural aspect of the cities. There aren't many Irani cafés left now, but in the remaining institutions, such as Britannia in south Mumbai, nothing has changed – high ceilings, bentwood chairs, chequerboard-tiled floors and marble tables. Dishoom, a well-known chain of Indian restaurants in the UK, pays homage to and is inspired by the old Irani café culture of Mumbai.

Makes 2 cups

2 cups water
2 cardamom pods (optional but recommended)
2 teaspoons tea leaves
2 teaspoons sugar, or according to taste
1½ cups milk
2 tablespoons condensed milk

Mix the water, cardamom pods, tea leaves and sugar in a saucepan. Bring to the boil, cover with a tight-fitting lid and let the tea simmer on a low heat for about 20 minutes. While the tea is brewing, boil the milk in another saucepan, then let it simmer until it reduces and thickens. Add the condensed milk and cook for a few more minutes, stirring regularly. Now strain the tea into a cup, add the milk mixture and stir together. Add more sugar as required.

Cinnamon Star Anise Chai

If you love cinnamon and liquorice, this is the tea for you. Star anise has a fragrant flavour, rather like liquorice. Both spices are great for digestion and the metabolism as well as for coughs and colds. You can also get star anise powder, also called Badian powder, which is concentrated, so you need less than ¼ teaspoon in your cup of chai. For optimal digestion and health, or if it's later in the day and you don't want caffeine, you could also make this tea simply with star anise, cinnamon and hot water.

Makes 1 cup

1 cup water
½ teaspoon ground cinnamon
2 whole star anise, or scant ¼ teaspoon Badian powder
1 teaspoon tea leaves
1 cup milk

Boil together all the ingredients except the milk, then add the milk once the water comes to a boil. Let this simmer for 3–5 more minutes. Switch to a high heat, let the tea rise to the top and reduce the heat. Do this a couple of times before straining into your cup.

Mumbai's Cutting Chai

In Mumbai, you'll find tapris (stalls) and chaiwalas selling small glass cups of Cutting Chai, Mumbai's lifeline, and so well known that if you just say 'cutting', anyone will know you mean chai. The name of the tea has a mysterious origin – some say it comes from 'cut in half', alluding to the small quantity of tea, or that it's so named because the chai is split in two cups, to be enjoyed in the company of friends; another theory is that the flavour is so strong that half a cup is plenty.

Makes 2 cups

2 whole cardamom pods
    or ¼ teaspoon cardamom powder
1 piece fresh ginger, grated
1 cup water
1 heaped teaspoon tea leaves
1½ teaspoons sugar
¾ cup milk

Crush the cardamom pods and ginger together in a pestle and mortar. Boil the water in a pan with the tea leaves, crushed ginger and cardamom, and the sugar. Bring to a boil on a high heat, then reduce the heat and simmer for a few minutes. Now add the milk and simmer for another 2–3 minutes on a low to medium heat. Strain into small serving cups.

Pumpkin Chai Latte

The pumpkin spice latte is a cultural icon, the orange colour symbolic of autumn leaves, and its warming spices, including cinnamon, ginger, nutmeg and clove recall pumpkin pie, served as part of Thanksgiving meals throughout the world. Launched by Starbucks in 2003, the recipe was originally developed by Peter Dukes, a college athlete and economist from Stanford University who joined the Starbucks team in 2001. It is now among the most popular seasonal beverages of all time and has taken on a life of its own, giving rise to an entire market of pumpkin spice products. The drink tastes just as delicious with tea as it does with the addition of coffee – so here's how to make the chai version. And if you want to leave the caffeine out altogether, you can make this with all the spices and pumpkin but omitting the tea or coffee.

Makes 1 cup

½ cup water
1 teaspoon loose tea leaves
small piece ginger, grated or crushed
1 cup milk
2 tablespoons pumpkin purée
1 tablespoon maple syrup or sugar
1 date, pitted and chopped
1 teaspoon cinnamon
¼ teaspoon or less nutmeg
pinch of salt

Boil the water with the tea leaves and ginger for around 5 minutes, then strain into another pan or into a cup, and put the strained liquid back into the pan. If you love the ginger kick, then keep the ginger strands or pieces in the pan so that you can blend this with the mixture. Now combine the strained liquid and the rest of the ingredients in a pan and boil on a low to medium heat. Transfer to a blender and blend until smooth. Taste and make any adjustments. Pour into cups. If you're making this without the tea leaves, you can simply blitz everything together in a high-speed blender, then pour into a pan and boil.

Chai story: After the rains

MARINE DRIVE, MUMBAI, 2011

Compared to the north of the city, which feels bustling, sticky and muggy, the roads are wider in the south, and there's more space to breathe, especially when walking along Marine Drive. This six-lane road, stretching along the coastline that forms a natural bay, is also known as the Queen's Necklace, because, when viewed at night from an elevated point along the drive, the lights resemble a string of pearls.

The view locks me into its serene magnificence each time I visit. You'll find people here every evening from all over the city, couples seeking a romantic moment, but also tourists, families, walkers and runners alike. I walk to Marine Drive from the iconic Oberoi Hotel, which has a breathtaking view of the entire Queen's Necklace from the swimming-pool balcony in the evening. I sigh as the balmy, warm evening air envelops me, a delicious relief from the air-conditioned hotels. I walk on the curved promenade by the sea, separated from the water by large rocks, the waves crashing lightly against them on my left while cars speed past on my right and a gentle breeze fans me. I pass families sitting by the water – a seating area above the rocks winds along the length of the curve – couples taking a stroll or an evening power walk, a group of men having a natter, clearly a daily habit, lovers with arms interlocked facing the water, or speaking as they stare into each other's eyes. The streetlights following the road stretch ahead of me, merging with Mumbai's skyline, which rises in the distance. And with the warm evening air compensating for the blistering heat in the day, I just want to carry on walking.

A little while later, I stop and sit next to what seems like a teenage brother and sister having a laugh with their mother. I see a man approaching, holding a bucket in one hand and calling 'Chai chai' as he approaches me. I haven't been to India in a while, and the old familiarity of the chaiwala's call plays on my memories. I've usually heard it when I'm on a train journey, stopping at a station where the call is a welcome lure out of my semi-slumbering state, as I wonder when the journey will end – in recent years, I've always opted for domestic flights, but there's something so unique about the train journey experience in India that I do miss it. In many instances, it is the train journey that has been etched on my memory more than anything else on my trips to India, something a little scary or funny that might have happened, from a group of ten of us friends somehow squashing into two cabins of four each, trying to dodge the ticket inspectors during the night, as there weren't enough spaces left on the train, to being alone in a first-class cabin with the man above me loudly farting all night. (I was meant to be in a women's cabin and didn't realise this.)

I watch the chaiwala pour chai for the mother while I sit and feel the warm breeze fan my face, the smell of rain hanging fresh in the air. It's a little late for tea and I had a streetside chai a few hours ago, so I decide to skip it now. Earlier in the day I had ventured to my favourite chaiwala, always stationed in the shade of a majestic old tree in Kala Godha, right outside the Sabyasachi flagship Mumbai store, which I love visiting just to admire the exquisite interiors. Sabyasachi is India's most famous fashion designer, who has collaborated with brands like Christian Louboutin and Pottery Barn and has played a significant role in taking Indian fashion to the global stage. Outside the Sabyasachi store, the chaiwala's stall sits under the shade of an old tree with a beautiful Shiva lingam* beside it, adorned with a fresh marigold garland, and a large Shiva Parvati and Ganesh image hanging from one of the boughs, seeming like an extension of the store itself. Sabyasachi may have nothing to do with the chai stall, which I first discovered many years ago after my first visit to his store, but there is something very spiritual and artistic about it.

I notice the string of slightly dried yellow limes and green chillies hanging above the Shiva lingam – something you'll see all over India, hanging outside homes, shops and on car grilles, which is believed to ward off evil spirits and bring luck and pros-

---

*   A Shiva lingam is an abstract representation of Lord Shiva, one of the principal deities in Hinduism. It is a cylindrical stone that is found in temples and homes and is worshipped as a symbol of creative energy and cosmic power. The shape of it is also believed to represent the union of the divine masculine and feminine energies, making it a powerful symbol of creation and regeneration.

perity. From a scientific or well-being perspective, lemon is sour and chilli is pungent, and thus they have insecticidal properties, keeping away flies and mosquitoes.

There's a constant stream of people here, standing and waiting to get their cup of replenishment, and so the chaiwala seems to continuously be pouring milk, grating ginger, adding scoops of sugar, boiling the tea until it froths, pouring it through a large strainer into another large pan, from the pan to an aluminium kettle, and then into small glasses with aplomb.

It's late now, past 11 p.m., and as I meander back, I walk on the other side of the Queen's Necklace, passing tall buildings rising above me and restaurants lining the drive. I give in to the temptation to have an ice-cream scoop from my go-to ice-cream shop, Natural, which always reminds me of family trips to Mumbai with my grandparents – my grandfather loved the flavours here: coconut, badam pista (almond and pistachio), anjir (fig) and sitaphal (custard fruit) when in season. In fact, staying at the Oberoi, which I rarely do now, reminds me of our trips with them – for two consecutive years, my parents had taken my grandparents to Mumbai, over a decade ago now, to stay at the Oberoi, have leisurely breakfasts, massages, an evening walk on Marine Drive and dinner at the local Gujarati thali restaurant called Status. During this month, we, meaning all the grandchildren and uncles and aunts, would come and go, for a few days or a week, and spend time with them. These were the trips when we would go to Natural together to get an ice cream in the evening, memories we cherish, and I know my grandmother remembers with fondness – her last few holidays with my grandfather.

I get a coconut scoop, always so fresh I can bite on the coconut flakes, and look up at the buildings lining Marine Drive as I walk back. The art deco buildings here are recognised by UNESCO as part of a World Heritage site along with the structures encircling *the sprawling Oval Maidan (the word 'maidan' meaning 'open space'), a large recreational ground and historic landmark in the heart of south Mumbai. Cricket and football are played here, and the structure showcases the different genres of Mumbai's architectural evolution, with its blend of old and new, traditional and modern. The eastern side is decked with neo-Gothic buildings (Mumbai University, Bombay High Court) with ornate spires and intricate stone carvings that are reminiscent of the Victorian era. The other side, where I'm walking this evening, features the more modernist style of architecture, iconic examples of art deco, overlooking the Arabian Sea, including the Eros Cinema, the New India Assurance Building and the Regal Cinema. The art deco buildings in Mumbai were primarily built in the 1930s, when India was still under British rule, and were influenced by the Hollywood film industry's glamorous style, characterised by bold geometric designs and decorative motifs such as sunbursts and zigzags. Mumbai is believed to have the second-most art deco buildings in the world, after Miami.*

On every trip to Mumbai, even though the nightlife, destination restaurants and all my friends are in the north of the city so I spend the majority of my time on that side, I make a point of staying at least a couple of nights in the south, usually alone. Walking around the south of Mumbai gives me a sense of the real Mumbai, of history, of beautiful architecture that isn't lost among the markets, vendors, people and shops, as it is in the north. Yet both sides of the city have their charm, and both are necessary to fulfil the true Bombay experience.

When I arrive back at my room at midnight, I head for a soak in the bathtub. On the way, I pick up a book lying on the coffee table, Mumbai Footpaths: Paths of Courage, Journeys of Hope, *little realising that my peek into this book would last an hour. What I read about the various Mumbai-ites' love of this city* engrossed me and almost made me long to discover all these secrets about Mumbai for myself. At almost two in the morning, I close the book, desperately wanting to spend another week in Mumbai. It will have to wait till next time.

Spiced Milk and Hot Chocolates

Badam Doodh
Masala Milk with Nuts

'Badam' are almonds and 'doodh' is milk, so this is a delicious sweet milk boiled with spices like saffron and cardamom as well as chopped nuts. It's an age-old Ayurvedic recipe we serve to guests on special occasions, and it's great for cold nights and good for kids, as it has spices, milk and nuts but no caffeine. It is drunk both hot or cooled, is garnished with sliced almonds and pistachios and sweetened with jaggery or sugar. Many recipes suggest soaking the almonds and blending them with the milk to make it creamy. However, I'm sharing the version of the recipe we've grown up drinking, the way my mother has always made it – delicious!

Makes 2 cups

2 cups milk
2 tablespoons brown sugar or jaggery
½ teaspoon ground cardamom or 3 cardamom pods, crushed
pinch of saffron strands, plus extra to garnish
1 tablespoon of almond flour (optional)
2 tablespoons chopped or sliced almonds
1 tablespoon chopped pistachios

Heat the milk in a saucepan on a low heat and add all the ingredients except the nuts. The almond flour will add richness, if you choose to add it. Simmer on a medium heat for 5–10 minutes so that the spices fully combine in the milk. Pour into cups and garnish with the chopped pistachios and almonds, and a few extra strands of saffron. If serving cold, leave the milk to cool down, then place in the fridge to chill and, when ready, pour into glasses with a few ice cubes.

Haldi Doodh
Turmeric Chai

The combination of turmeric and milk is incredibly nourishing for the body and it is often recommended to drink this chai before bed. Turmeric chai, also known as golden milk, not only improves sleep quality, but is also a lovely ritual to incorporate into your evening routine. Adding spices like ginger, cinnamon, cardamom and pepper to this milk make it more aromatic and flavourful. Adding a pinch of black pepper to your turmeric is not only a great way to add warmth to your golden milk, but also nutritionally beneficial. Pepper contains a compound called piperine, which can help your body absorb curcumin, the active component in turmeric. Curcumin has been found to boost mood and alleviate symptoms of depression; it inhibits molecules that cause inflammation in the body, in turn helping to boost immunity; and it's been found to regulate blood-sugar levels and other health-related issues associated with diabetes. If drinking this at bedtime, add ¼ teaspoon ground nutmeg and a pinch of saffron.

Makes 1 cup

1 cup milk
½ teaspoon ground turmeric
¼ teaspoon ground ginger or fresh ginger, grated
½ teaspoon ground cinnamon
a pinch of ground black pepper
1 teaspoon jaggery or any sugar you like (optional)
¼ teaspoon ground nutmeg (optional)
a pinch of saffron (optional)

Boil together all the ingredients and stir on a low to medium heat for a few minutes. Once boiled, pour into a cup.

Kesar Doodh
Saffron Bedtime Milk

I love the subtle flavour and warmth of saffron – and while it's one of the most expensive spices, a little goes a long way! Various studies have shown the positive effect of saffron on sleep. It is also rich in antioxidants, can help improve mood and thus help those with depression. Adding nutmeg to this drink further aids sleep, working as a natural sedative. Nutmeg also stimulates the release of serotonin, which creates a feeling of calmness.

Makes 1 cup

1 cup milk
a pinch of saffron
¼ teaspoon ground nutmeg
1 teaspoon brown sugar or jaggery (optional)

Boil together all the ingredients in a pan on a medium heat for a few minutes. Pour into a mug.

Iced Chai Milk

This is a luxurious yet refreshing drink, made by blending together milk with a boiled tea concoction and additional chai spices. The dates give a lovely caramel-like flavour. If you want to make this creamier and richer, add some almond butter or peanut butter when blending.

Tea concentrate:
½ cup water
1 teaspoon tea leaves or a teabag
1 teaspoon grated ginger or ¼ teaspoon ginger powder

For blending:
1 cup milk
1 teaspoon cinnamon powder
¼ teaspoon cardamom powder
few saffron strands (optional)
2 dates, pitted
pinch of salt
a few ice cubes

Boil together the ingredients for the tea concentrate for a few minutes on a medium heat until the colour of the water is a dark brown. Once boiled, pour through a strainer if you have used loose tea leaves; if using a teabag, simply remove it.

Put the tea concentrate with the rest of the ingredients into a high-speed blender, and blend. Taste and make any adjustments. If it's not sweet enough, you can add another date or even some honey.

Put the ice cubes into a large glass and pour over the blended milk.

Ukaro
Masala Milk

While I grew up drinking ukaro, which is chai without the tea leaves, I still have this today when I'm having a chai later in the day and I don't want any caffeine. It is made by boiling milk with the chai spice blend or whole spices and sugar. My chai brand is in fact this – a blend of coconut sugar and spices – and in many cafés where you order chai latte, you may even find this: masala milk rather than a masala chai. As a child I would drink it with toast or puris, made by my grandmother on weekend mornings; on school mornings, it was always simple porridge and no drinks. I still remember dipping my hot, buttered toast in the milky ukaro to get a slightly crispy, slightly soggy texture, or soaking my fresh, soft and slightly crisp puri in the ukaro and sucking or slurping the sweet milk before taking a bite of the puri. You can either use your favourite chai spice mix (see page 79 for my family's) or crush whole spices and boil them in milk.

Makes 1 cup

Using your home chai spice mixture:
¾ cup milk
½ cup water
¼ teaspoon chai masala mix (spice blend from page 79)
1–2 teaspoons jaggery or sugar

Boil together all the ingredients on a medium heat, then switch to a high heat so that it boils well, and then reduce it again to a low to medium heat. Do this a few times to ensure the spices dissolve well into the milk. Taste and make any adjustments, then pour into your cup. Note: You can use less or more of the chai spice mixture as required. If you don't have your own ready mix and want to use ground spices, simply add ¼ teaspoon cardamom, less than ¼ teaspoon cinnamon and a pinch of ginger.

> *Using whole spices:*
> 1 small cinnamon stick
> 1–2 whole cardamom pods
> ½ inch / 1cm chunk ginger
> 1 clove
> 2 peppercorns
> ½ cup water
> 1 teaspoon jaggery
> ¾ cup milk

Grind the spices in a pestle and mortar so that they are loose and broken. This will allow the spices to absorb into the water easily. Put them into a pan with the water and jaggery and boil for around 5 minutes. Add the milk and let this boil for a few more minutes. Strain into a cup.

Tip: If you're making this for a child, omit the peppercorns and use less ginger so it is less spicy, but a mild level of spices is great for kids, especially in the winter months.

Winter Spiced Hot Chocolate with Melted Dark Chocolate

As I write this, I'm sipping on this incredible hot chocolate and have to stop myself from making another one. It's like chocolate soup – thick, velvety and rich. I've made it with 70 per cent dark chocolate and it has a few spices to enhance the flavour and add that lovely warmth. Remember, each spice has a number of health benefits, so you're boosting the nutritional value by adding spices. I love the combination of chocolate and ginger, but I've added cardamom as well as cinnamon and vanilla here – you can use whichever you like. It all tastes delicious together! Cocoa is rich in antioxidants and, since dark chocolate contains more cocoa, it has higher levels of antioxidants than milk chocolate. Cocoa also contains tryptophan, which is an amino acid the brain uses to make serotonin, known as the 'happy hormone'.

Makes 1 cup

1 cup milk
⅓ cup/40g dark chocolate (70 per cent cocoa solids),
     roughly broken into small pieces
½ teaspoon cocoa powder
¼ teaspoon ginger powder
¼ teaspoon cardamom powder
¼ teaspoon cinnamon powder
½ teaspoon vanilla essence
a pinch of sea salt

Heat half the milk in a pan and when it starts boiling add all the chocolate, stir until it melts, then add the rest of the milk and keep stirring. Now add the cocoa powder and all the spices, vanilla essence and salt and keep stirring. If you have a hand-held milk frother, use this to mix and froth the hot chocolate, then pour into your cup.

Chai story: My grandparents' yatra

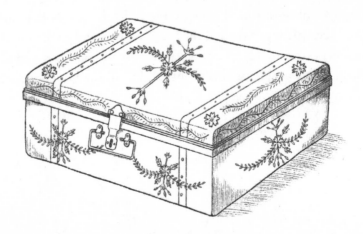

When their children, my dad and uncles, were young boys aged two, four and seven, my grandparents Bhabhi and Babhai (somehow Prabhudasbhai had turned into Babhai, and just like Bhabhi's name, Babhai is what we all called him, rather than the traditional word for grandfather, 'Dada') decided to leave their small home in Uganda and embark on an eight-month-long trip to India. My grandfather was born in Uganda and had never been to India, and for my grandmother, this was her first visit since leaving her grandmother's village with her father. This trip to India was their version of a yatra (pilgrimage to the homeland), a type of journey that was common in their generation, although no one they knew had done this for so long, let alone with three very young children in tow.

The trip included visiting pilgrimage sites as well as meeting family members, including Bhabhi's grandmother, who she hadn't seen since she left for Africa as a teenager. My grandparents arrived in India a decade after independence, in 1957, to a new India, but Bhabhi said nothing seemed too different, especially in the villages. Mostly, they stayed at dharamasalas (shelters for pilgrims), where accommodation and meals were free. Breakfast would include the chai they were given at the dharamsala. I ask Bhabhi about her most memorable chai on this trip, assuming she may not have an answer, but, to my surprise, she does. She remembers because it was the first time she had had chai in a traditional 'maati' clay cup (also known as a 'kulhad' cup). A maati is handle-less and provides an earthy aroma to the drink because the cups are unglazed and therefore the tea partially soaks into the interior wall of the cup, enhancing the flavour and fragrance.

Bhabhi had this chai at a train station en route from Ahmedabad in Gujarat to Haridwar in the north of India and then onwards to Dehradun. They had to stop at a station called Mehsana to change trains, and it was already midnight, past everyone's bedtime, and they had a few hours to wait until their train arrived. The boys were falling asleep and so she lay all three of them down on their one family suitcase – the only trunk they carried between them for the whole eight months, which my grandfather carried everywhere – put a blanket they had with them over the boys, and they fell asleep immediately. Mehsana is still in Gujarat, so this must have been a few hours into their two-day train journey, maybe even longer, Bhabhi says. Today, the journey from Ahmedabad to Haridwar takes twenty-five hours.

Arriving at a station and drinking chai was a welcome break, a one-rupee cup of sustenance from a young boy walking around with a large urn. What was memorable about this chai, Bhabhi tells me, aside from the cup, was that it had lots of ginger, was very milky and that, soon after, when they were catching the next train, my dad closed the door on my uncle's hand, so the memory is tied to this, to holding her youngest, two-year-old son tight until he stopped crying. 'We didn't have plasters or medication,' she says, when I asked what she did. 'We just had to make do.' I do wonder how much we would be packing if we were taking even one child to India today – to think they had one trunk between them, and on their journey back, my grandfather had one extra thing in his hand – he was carrying a beautiful marble 'murti' or deity of goddess Amba Maa, which my grandmother had fallen in love with. It remains in her temple room to this day – from Gujarat to Uganda to London. She still sits and prays every morning and night, leaves a small steel bowl of cashews and shakkar, or rock sugar, by Maa's feet as prasad (an offering), which is then eaten by anyone in the house; and at any family occasion, we bow to her to get blessings.

At another railway station in the Mehsana district, called Vadnagar, the current Prime Minister of India Narendra Modi sold tea as a child with his father, probably around the same time. And it was also around this time that the CTC (Crush, Tear, and Curl) machines (see page 124) had started revolutionising the tea industry in India, automating the tea-making process and bringing down the cost of tea.

Indian Coffee

Filter Coffee

Coffee in India is defined by south Indian filter coffee, known as 'filter kaapi', but this is not filter coffee the way we know it in the West. South Indian filter coffee is hot and milky, with foamy bubbles always seated on top of the steel cups in which it is served, which are placed in containers known as dabarah (meaning container or cup) that are used to cool and mix the coffee.

Coffee has in fact been grown by Indians since the sixteenth century, and was first brought to India by Baba Budan, a Muslim saint from Chikmagalur, who is said to have smuggled seven coffee beans from present-day Yemen while returning from a pilgrimage to Mecca. We think of tea as quintessentially Indian, but coffee too has a long, distinguished history on the subcontinent, and it dates back even further than tea-drinking. Indian filter coffee does, however, require specialised equipment and some skill to make.

It is made in stainless steel filters, synonymous with Indian filter coffee. The filter consists of two halves that resemble cylindrical cups, onto one of which fresh grounds are loaded and pressed. Then water is poured slowly or rather trickled onto it, while the other half collects the filtered coffee. The hot milk and sugar is then added and it is the pouring of the coffee between the filter and the dabarah that creates the classic frothy layer over the filter coffee.

Given that most people reading this book won't have an Indian filter coffee maker, I'm going to suggest using an Italian

Bialetti in which you can make your coffee the way you would normally make it, and boil the milk and sugar, if using, separately.

Makes 2 cups – using a Bialetti for 2

1½–2 tablespoons filter coffee powder,
   however strong you like it
½ cup milk
2 teaspoons sugar or jaggery, to taste

Start by making the filter coffee decoction, in the way you would normally make espresso in a Bialetti. In a saucepan, boil the milk and sugar or jaggery. Pour the coffee, once brewed, into the tumblers or cups, then pour in the hot milk and try to pour quickly from one cup to the other to achieve the classic froth layer on top. Alternatively, you can use a milk frother to do this.

The results may vary depending on the type of coffee you use and the strength of decoction you like.

This method achieves a similar result to Indian filter coffee, but do visit a South Indian restaurant at breakfast time, anywhere in the world, and you'll most likely be able to get a perfectly made filter coffee, served in the traditional stainless steel cup and dabarah.

Masala Coffee

This herbal coffee brew comes from South India and is a medic-inal pick-me-up and a delicious winter warmer, healing for colds and congestion and good for digestion. The recipe uses ground spices and mineral-rich jaggery, usually boiled in water, but you can also add milk if you like. I would call the milky version a masala coffee, but it's more commonly known in the West as Dirty Chai or Dirty Chai Latte. In either case, it's just chai spices added to a shot of coffee! Here's how to make this at home with whole spices, giving a potent flavour and aroma.

Makes 1 cup

1 small cinnamon stick
1–2 whole cardamoms
½ inch / 1cm chunk ginger
2 cloves
1 peppercorn/a sprinkle of black pepper
a few tulsi or holy basil leaves, if you have them
1 cup water
1 teaspoon jaggery
¼ cup milk (optional)
1 teaspoon instant coffee

Grind the spices in a pestle and mortar so they are loose and broken. This will allow the spices to absorb into the water easily. Now boil the water with the spices and add the jaggery. Add the milk if using. Let this boil for 5 minutes or longer. Add the coffee to your cup, pour the spice brew into the cup through a strainer and stir well.

Chai story: Mount Kailas

Travelling to and staying close to the sacred Mount Kailas for nine days in August 2011 was my most profound, memorable and sacred trip. It was summer in Kailas, such a beautiful time to venture into the Himalayas, shrouded in warmth and sunshine during the day, turning into crisp, cool and dark evenings. The brilliance of the moon lit up the entire silhouette of Mount Kailas each night, and allowed the water running in the stream beside us, separating our camp from Kailas, to sparkle and glisten. The mountain seemed to be alive and breathing, so large that it felt near, yet entirely untouched. Shrouded in mystery, central to tales of Lord Shiva, Mount Kailas is the spiritual epicentre of not one but four different religions – Buddhism, Hinduism, Jainism and Bon (the precursor to Buddhism). One thing all the religions hold

sacred is a prohibition against climbing the peak. It is believed that Mount Kailas holds the axis of life and death, for Lord Shiva, who resides here, is the god of creation and destruction.

I made chai for Bapu, our spiritual leader, daily and, as I walked out of the makeshift kitchen, I would see Mount Kailas before me. We stayed in the foothills of the mountain, beside the flowing stream of water, listening to its trickling music as we fell asleep each night, for nine days. Many make the journey to Mount Kailas to perform parikrama (circumambulation), which takes three days, the ultimate pilgrimage for a Hindu, but we were here for Bapu's Ram Katha, a nine-day recital of the Ram Charit Manas, *Tulsidasji's version of the* Ramayana *epic. Staying here for nine days required years of planning and gaining permission from the Chinese government, as it has never happened in the history of this mountain – permission was granted for only 300 listeners, a far cry from the hundreds of thousands that attend Bapu's Ram Katha events in India.*

Travelling to the mountain itself is a feat. Kailas sits in the remote far western hinterlands of Tibet, in the part of the Tibetan Himalayas that is under Chinese jurisdiction. Luckily, the roads are smoother and easier to drive on than in earlier years, but travellers still needed to stop along the way and acclimatise to the altitude at various points, with those unable to bear the effects of the elevation forced to turn back. On my trip, we were lucky with the weather, but depending on the time of year, it can also switch from cold to freezing in minutes.

In the mornings, Bapu would drink the chai I had made quickly, as was his custom, from a patra (wooden bowl), slurping each piping-hot sip before the temperature dropped even slightly. With this, he would have his breakfast, sometimes thepla, sometimes fresh ganthia and marcha (fresh green fried chillies) and sometimes rotlo and dahi (millet flour roti and home-made *curd). He would then recite the* Ram Charit Manas *for three hours, a discourse about the scripture itself, about life and spirituality and other topics. There were a number of people who fell ill and had to head back to Kathmandu early and, during the nine days, one of Bapu's brothers suddenly fell ill and passed away – it was a testing, unexpected time.*

I could give you endless descriptions of Mount Kailas, ever metamorphosing, how its form and shape seemed to alter each day, each hour. In the morning the peak would hide behind opaque mist and then thrust from layers of white and grey until all but whispers of cloud disappeared and Kailas dazzled with white intensity, ethereal. Then, as the clouds stood marshalled further away in the afternoon, the mountain would be bathed in the brilliance of the sun, until the early evening hours often brought waves of grey rainclouds, and Kailas once again took cover and retreated into its celestial respite. On some nights, though, the sky would be a blanket of shining stars, with Mount Kailas hiding in the thick blackness of the night.

When I left Kailas, heading down into the small town of Darchen, I realised I was not ready to be in touch with the world again. I wasn't ready to be on earth. And whether it was being in the midst of mountains, in this higher spiritual realm, or whether it was the disconnection, time spent without a phone, email, anything, in isolation from the real world, I felt as though I was somewhere not classified as earth, somewhere so close to the sun, clouds and stars that it felt most heavenly.

Herbal Teas

Ayurvedic Tea Blend

This is a very simple blend of three whole spices – coriander, cumin and fennel – mixed together in equal amounts. You can place this in a jar and boil daily with hot water. In Ayurveda, everything centres around the gut and everything leads back to the gut. This tea supports the gut, can be drunk by anyone, can help with bloating, flatulence, gas and soothe any abdominal pain. It can also help with sinus issues and is suitable for any time of day. By boiling the spices, they are able to release their medicinal properties into the hot water.

> 2 tablespoons cumin seeds
> 2 tablespoons coriander seeds
> 2 tablespoons fennel seeds

Mix together the spices and store in a jar. When you want to drink the tea, boil together 2 cups of hot water with 1 teaspoon of the spice mix. You can also make a larger amount, keep it in a jug and sip warm or cool for the rest of the day. I like chewing on the seeds while drinking the tea, but if you prefer tea without the seeds, strain them and use them again for another cup, if you like.

Tip: Add ajwain or carom (caraway) seeds to this spice mixture for extra digestive benefit and if you're suffering from a cold, flu or sinus issues. This gives it a stronger and spicier taste, but has a whole host of benefits, including aiding weight loss and lowering blood pressure.

Kashmiri Kahwa

This traditional Kashmiri tea or kahwa is made with green tea leaves and flavoured with cardamom, cloves, cinnamon, saffron and rose petals. Kashmiris refer to kahwa as Mogul chai, a tea that was introduced by the Mughal emperors. It's a popular drink throughout Kashmir, Afghanistan, Central Asia, Iran and the Middle East.

Saffron grows abundantly and almond trees thrive in Kashmir, so a kahwa is always topped with slivered almonds. It is said to help burn the fat and warm the body in the cold climate of Kashmir. This tea is rich in antioxidants, boosts the metabolism and is a good remedy for coughs and colds, perfect for cold winters. It was traditionally prepared in a copper kettle, or samovar, which had a central cavity into which live coals were placed to keep the tea hot. Locals here also drink noon chai, which literally translates as salt tea; and as the name suggests, they add salt instead of sugar, along with green tea leaves and a pinch of sodium bicarbonate, turning the tea a pink colour.

Makes 1 mug or 2 cups

2 cups boiling water
1 cinnamon stick
2 cardamom pods, opened and crushed if possible
2 cloves
a few dried rose petals
a pinch of saffron strands
1 teaspoon green tea leaves
1 tablespoon slivered almonds or almond flour
2 teaspoons jaggery or honey

Pour the boiling water in a pan (or boil the water), add the cinnamon stick, cardamom pods, cloves, rose petals and saffron. Let this boil for 2 minutes, then add the green tea leaves and heat for a few more minutes on a low to medium heat. While this is cooking, put the almond slivers or almond flour in your serving mug or cups and add another small pinch of saffron (2 or 3 strands). Pour the boiled mixture through a strainer into your mug or cups, add jaggery or honey and enjoy.

Kadha

A hot cup of kadha, a traditional Ayurvedic decoction of herbs and spices, is soothing, warming and healing, especially in the winter months or if you have a cough or cold. Like masala chai, kadha is made in different ways and you can use whichever spices you have. The peppercorns and ginger give warmth and spice, while the cinnamon and jaggery sweeten the mixture. It helps reduce mucus, soothes the throat and helps reduce inflammation.

If you have tulsi plants or tulsi leaves at home, these are beneficial for digestion, the respiratory passages and stress. If you don't have tulsi, either leave this out or use mint leaves instead. Cloves and black pepper are known to act as an expectorant and thus help loosen mucus. Honey balances the flavours and has anti-inflammatory properties.

1 mug or 2 cups

2 cloves
1 cinnamon stick
a pinch of coarsely ground black pepper or
    a few peppercorns
½ inch/1cm piece of ginger, grated, or chopped
    into pieces, or ¼ teaspoon ground ginger
5–7 tulsi leaves (holy basil)
2½ cups water
a pinch of salt
2 teaspoons jaggery or honey

Heat a saucepan, add the cloves, cinnamon, pepper, ginger and tulsi leaves and dry-roast on a slow flame for around 30 seconds. Add the water and salt, mix well and heat on a medium flame for around 10 minutes (the water will reduce down a little). Strain the mixture into a mug, add the jaggery or honey and mix well.

Variyari nu Pani

This is a drink I've grown up with, cooling sweet fennel water. Whenever the sun came out, my grandmother would prepare a jug of this and leave it in the fridge. It's refreshing, quenches the thirst and leaves you wanting more, especially when it's really hot. This is also served as a refreshment by the bride's family to the groom's family when they arrive for a wedding, a tradition that probably began in India due to the heat, but is still carried out at most Indian weddings anywhere in the world. Traditionally the drink is sweetened with sugar crystals called 'misri' or 'rock sugar', said to be the purest form of sugar, with numerous health benefits, according to Ayurveda. These crystals gently dissolve in the water, while the fennel powder is also soaking through and infusing the water. If you don't have misri, however, you can use agave or sugar.

Makes 6–8 glasses

4 tablespoons fennel powder
1 litre water
3 tablespoons/80g misri or sugar

You will also need:
a muslin cloth
a rubber band

Place the fennel powder in the muslin cloth and tie it with a rubber band or simply knot it to prevent the powder escaping. Place in a large jug with the measured water and misri and stir so the flavour can infuse through the cloth.

Leave to soak for 4–5 hours at least, either in a cool place or in the fridge (it can also be left overnight). Remove the muslin bag from the water, check that all the misri has melted, and strain the water from the bag for full flavour and no waste. Stir well and serve. The water will have a light green colour.

Sulaimani Tea

Black teas and teas brewed with spices are an ancient tradition in the Arab world, and sulaimani tea is a great example of the intermingling of cultures. The Arab word 'sulaiaman' means 'man of peace' and this tea was introduced to the Malabar coast by Arab traders. This spiced black tea, made without milk and brewed to a golden colour with spices and a squeeze of lemon, is still most popular in the Malabar region of south-west India.

Makes 1 mug or 2 cups

1–2 cardamom pods
1 cinnamon stick
1 or 2 cloves
½ inch/1cm piece ginger, grated or chopped
2½ cups water
1 teaspoon tea leaves
2 teaspoons lemon juice
2 teaspoons jaggery, sugar or honey

Use a pestle and mortar to crush the spices. If you have grated the ginger, you don't need to grind this. Now add the spices to the water in a pan and boil for a few minutes until the spices become infused in the water. Add the tea leaves and lemon juice and boil for longer on a low to medium heat. Pour into your cup or mug through a sieve and stir in the jaggery or sugar or honey.

Alcohol-free Mulled Wine

This warming spicy drink combines citrus with spice and sweetness, fresh fruit with the delicious aromas of cinnamon sticks, star anise, nutmeg and cloves – truly it is Christmas in a cup.

Makes 4 small cups

1 tablespoon grated ginger
1 cup water
3–4 small cinnamon sticks
¼ teaspoon cinnamon powder
3 cloves
2 whole star anise
a pinch of nutmeg
¼ teaspoon turmeric powder
1 large orange or 2 small oranges
1 lime or lemon
2 tablespoons honey or any sweetener you like
a handful cranberries

Boil the grated ginger in water and let this boil for a few minutes before straining into another pan. (If you like to chew the ginger pieces, then leave the ginger in the same pan.) Add the cinnamon sticks, cinnamon powder, cloves, star anise, nutmeg and turmeric into the ginger water and squeeze in the juice from the citrus fruits. I like to squeeze them with my hands, using a knife to scrape out as much of the pulp as I can. Stir in the honey or sugar once boiled, before tasting and making any adjustments. Now stir in the cranberries or add to each glass when serving.

Lemon Iced Tea

A classic iced tea – zesty, refreshing, and the perfect blend of sweet and citrus. You can even have it without sugar. It's great for the summer months, especially for picnics, and is something you can make quickly and easily with lots of variations.

Makes 1 large glass or 2 small glasses

1 teaspoon tea leaves
1 cup water
juice of ½ a lemon
a few ice cubes
2 teaspoons sugar
mint leaves for garnishing (optional)

Boil the tea leaves in the water, then let this cool. Pour the lemon juice in a glass, add the ice cubes and sugar and pour over the cooled, brewed tea. You can also leave this in the fridge for a while or overnight. Garnish with the mint leaves, if using, before serving.

Iced Saffron Lime or Lemon

This simple concoction makes for a perfect summer's drink, luxuriously cooling and colourful. It's great for a small picnic or as a welcome drink at home. I've added honey for a touch of sweetness, but you can add any sweetener or some coconut sugar, and a little less or more according to taste. I like this without tea leaves, but you can make the iced-tea version of this by simply boiling tea leaves in the water with the saffron and lime or lemon.

Makes 2 cups

1½ cups water
juice of 1 lime or lemon
pinch of saffron
3 tablespoons sugar or honey
a few ice cubes
mint leaves for garnishing

Boil the water, lime juice and saffron for a few minutes until the water turns a golden orange hue. Let this cool down, then add the sugar or honey and stir well. Pour over ice, garnish with the mint leaves, and drink.

Chai story: Mahashivratri Mela

Junagadh, Gujurat, 2005

It's past midnight as I walk with my friend from London, Sonal, through the lively lanes of Laldhori, a large forest area near the Bhavnath temple where the Mahashivratri mela (festival) takes place every February. It's the second-largest religious gathering in India after the Kumbh mela. Most years, my guru, Morari Bapu, spends the few days of the mela here, and I've joined the group of pilgrims surrounding him. With about a million devotees attending the mela, it's not a place you would navigate alone, especially as a woman, and so, getting to go as part of a group was a very unique experience.*

During the nights, music and 'bhajans', the sounds of devotional celebrations, held in large open tents, fill the air until the early hours of the morning. I pass hundreds of people sitting in

---

*   With Hinduism following the lunar calendar, all festivals change dates, but Mahashivratri is usually in February.

each tent, listening to and singing along with the folk singer or priest on stage. We enter one of the tents, where my friend knows the artist performing, and so we walk to the front and sit down. I sing along to a familiar folk song. A few people from the front and back walk through the crowd to throw money in the air above the artist, a traditional way to show appreciation, which adds to the theatrical pizazz and cultural effervescence of the night.

I notice a man at the end of the row handing out rakabis (saucers), into which he pours chai. Luckily, there are tiny plastic cups too – the rakabis look rather stained and wet. My friend tells me that after use they just dip the saucers into a large bucket to clean them, without changing the water. Two days in, I'm still not accustomed to using the hole-in-the-ground toilet and sleeping on the rather dusty and smelly cushions in our guest house. Although I've done this many times in India, when I travel to smaller towns and villages for kathas,* the toilets never seem to get easier to deal with – especially when you get even the mildest form of food poisoning.

When the chai comes round to us, the man serving it seems to realise we're from abroad and hands us both the plastic cups. 'Thank you,' I shout, as he pours the chai. He fills it hallway and a little froth of bubbles settles atop. It's kadak, a dark milky brew, and very sweet, a shot of caffeine and sugar to keep the audience awake into the early hours.

Mahashivratri is one of the most significant spiritual nights in the Hindu calendar, a celebration of Lord Shiva, known as the creator and the destroyer of the universe. Some believe this is the

---

* My guru does nine-day Ram Kathas, or spiritual recitals, around the world and around India – I usually go once a year and, when I was younger, I would be happy attending whichever katha was going on during my school holidays. Sometimes they just happened to be in the small villages and towns of India, where we had to make to do with the facilities.

day when Lord Shiva saved the world by drinking poison that emerged from the ocean during Samudra Manthan. This poison got stored in his throat, making it blue, which is the reason that Lord Shiva is also known as Neelkanth (Blue Throat). Others believe that Mahashivratri is the wedding night of Lord Shiva to his consort Parvati, or that this is the night that Lord Shiva, as the Lord of the Dance or Nataraja, performed the Tandava dance, the cosmic dance of creation, destruction and preservation.

The night of Mahashivratri falls on the night before the full moon, on chaudas, the fourteenth of the month in the lunar month of Phalgun, usually in February. Hundreds of thousands of followers, including sadhus (holy men), folk singers and Shiva devotees from all over India flock to Laldhori, a forest at the foothills of the Girnar range in Gujarat in the days leading up to Mahashivratri. By day, there are stalls with piles of rudraksha malas (necklaces of japa beads) in all colours and sizes; there are hundreds of food and chai stalls and areas where thalis are given for free, large kitchens making multitudes of everything from roti and daal to bhajiya and samosa. The sadhus, India's wandering holy men, also known as naga bavas, roam around, some with long beards that touch their navels and long, matted dreadlocks hanging or wrapped in a bun. Most are fully naked except for large rudraksha malas hanging around their necks, some wear garlands of marigolds; their bodies are covered in ash or bhasma, which looks like a pasty white, chalk-like paint, prepared by burning a mix of cow dung and ghee several times to get a fine powder. These sadhus have renounced worldly life, giving up possessions and families to lead a life of celibacy and search for enlightenment. Resembling the form of Lord Shiva, they are considered representatives of Shiva himself and revered. You'll frequently spot them smoking marijuana using a chillum pipe, inhaling intently and blowing out large clouds of smoke, a daily ritual connected with Lord Shiva – charas (cannabis concentrate) is venerated by some as being one of the aspects of the god.

The main event occurs at 9 p.m. on the final night, the night of Mahashivratri in full moon, when the ash-smeared bavas march in a religious procession for three hours, seated on elephants, holding flags and blowing conch shells as they move towards the temple to participate in the puja, or worship ritual, performed at midnight. Before the puja, they take a ritualistic bath in the Mrigi Kund (water tank) at the Bhavnath temple at midnight, as many of them as possible going in at once, immersing their entire bodies and heads and jumping up quickly. It is firmly believed that Lord Shiva himself visits the shrine on this occasion.

It is difficult to get into the area of the Bhavnath temple at this time to witness this, amidst the hundreds and thousands of people. One year, my dad, who was with me during one of the melas I attended, said that he and a cameraman were part of a BBC crew. And we therefore scurried through the crowds and managed to watch the bavas jumping into the kund at midnight, as the rhythms and beats of bhajans peaked. My guru usually sits alone in maun (silence), in his own quiet camp area, the music echoing in the distance. For Bapu, Shiva signifies atma (soul), Shiva signifies compassion, Shiva signifies stillness.

Lassis

Yoghurt is naturally cooling for the body, which is why yoghurt drinks, made in all sorts of different ways, abound in the hotter regions of the world – chaas or lassi in India, laban in Turkey, ayran in the Middle East. The one thing that remains constant for the Indian salted version is ground cumin. Rather like chai, lassi is traditionally served in a clay cup known as a kulhad or kulhar cup. At home, we make a slightly lighter version of lassi with buttermilk, which in Gujarati we call chaas. As it's less heavy, this drink pairs well with an Indian meal or thali, especially kitchari (kedgeree).

Lassi with Ginger and Coriander

Makes 2 cups

1½ teaspoons ground cumin or cumin seeds
8 tablespoons natural yoghurt
1½ cups water
1 teaspoon salt, ideally Himalayan
a handful coriander leaves, chopped
1 inch piece of peeled, grated ginger

If using cumin seeds, roast them in a pan for a minute or until you smell the aroma, not letting them burn. Then blend all the ingredients until smooth using a wire whisk or a high-speed blender, pour into a jug and refrigerate. This should last 2–3 days in the fridge.

Lassi with Mint

This version of lassi is very popular in the northern region of Punjab, where field workers replenish and cool themselves with mint lassi, often made with both sugar and salt. Mint calms the stomach, helps with bloating, is a mouth refresher and cools the body. This lassi pairs very well with spicy food.

Makes 2 cups

8 tablespoons yoghurt
1½ cups water
1 teaspoon salt, ideally Himalayan
1 teaspoon ground cumin or cumin seeds
a handful (around 20–25) mint leaves
6–8 ice cubes

Blend all the ingredients until smooth, pour into a jug and leave in refrigerator. This should last 2–3 days in the fridge.

Lassi with Tadka

This is lassi with a ghee or oil 'tempering' (fried spices and curry leaves) poured into the mixture. It's popular in Gujarat, especially in the region of Kathiawad, where my family is from. My paternal grandfather, who I grew up with and who passed away only two years ago, used to love drinking this, right up until his very last days, especially with a simple kichri meal – kichri is a blend of rice and mung beans boiled and cooked in water until until it reaches a frothy, liquidy consistency, stirred with ghee or served with a simple curry, and the most balanced meal, according to Ayurveda. Ayurvedically, since this lassi also has cooked spices, it is better for the digestion.

Makes 2 glasses

For the lassi:
1 cup natural yoghurt or buttermilk
2 cups water
1 tablespoon coriander leaves, chopped
1 teaspoon cumin powder
around ½ teaspoon salt

For the tempering:
½ teaspoon ghee or oil
½ teaspoon cumin seeds
1 small green chilli, finely chopped
8–10 curry leaves

Use a hand whisk to thoroughly mix together the ingredients for the lassi in a bowl. Now make the tempering. Heat the ghee or oil in a small pan, add the cumin, green chilli and then the curry leaves. Let them crackle for a few seconds, then pour into the lassi. You can pour it into glasses and drink immediately, or it will keep for around 3 days in the fridge in a covered jug or glasses.

Lassi with Rose and Cardamom

A refreshing yet floral and dessert-like drink, combining two ingredients that pair beautifully together (there's a chai on page 99 made with rose and cardamom too). If you want to make this look classic rose pink, use pink rose syrup. Using syrup will also add a delicious sweetness to the drink. If using almonds, ideally use soaked almonds, as they will be easier to blend and digest. Either boil them for 10–20 minutes on a medium heat or simply soak them overnight. You can remove the skin if you like.

Makes 2 glasses

5 tablespoons natural yoghurt
2 teaspoons rose water or rose syrup (see page 98)
¼ teaspoon ground cardamom
½ cup water
1 tablespoon sugar
1 tablespoon almond flour or 5–7 almonds

Optional garnish:
dried rose petals

Mix together all the ingredients and blitz in a high-speed blender. If it's too thick, you can add more water; add more yoghurt if you want to thicken it. You can also add a little more almond flour to thicken it. Pour into small glasses and add cubes of ice if you like.

Mango Lassi

This delicious sweet lassi has become incredibly popular and you'll find it at many of your favourite Indian restaurants. Alphonso mangoes make the best lassi as they're incredibly sweet, but you can use any mangoes you like, either fresh, frozen or even canned mango pulp. Traditionally plain yoghurt or curd is used to make mango lassi, so if you're using Greek yoghurt, which is thicker, you may need to add some extra milk to get the right consistency. Mango lassi often includes milk as well as yoghurt, but you can use water instead of the milk if you prefer. Cardamom really brings that Indian flavour to the lassi.

Makes 2 large glasses

1 small or medium ripe mango
½ cup/4 tablespoons yoghurt
1 cup milk
1½ tablespoons honey or sugar
½ teaspoon ground cardamom
a handful ice cubes

Optional garnishes:
chopped pistachios
a few saffron strands

Blend together all the ingredients and make any adjustments to the consistency, adding more milk to make it thinner, or more yoghurt to thicken. If the mangoes are not sweet enough, you can add more honey or sugar. Garnish with pistachios and saffron strands.

Vegan Mango Lassi

Makes 2 glasses

1 small or medium ripe mango
1 cup coconut milk
2 tablespoons coconut cream
¾ teaspoon ground cardamom
1 tablespoon honey
a few ice cubes

Optional garnishes:
chopped pistachios
a few saffron strands

Blend together the ingredients – mango, coconut milk, coconut cream, cardamom, honey and ice cubes – in a high-speed blender. Taste and adjust the sweetness and flavour by adding more honey or cardamom. Pour into glasses and sprinkle with pistachios and saffron, if using.

Fennel Chia Smoothie

This is a rich, decadent smoothie, thickened with cashews and almond butter. The fennel powder gives it a delicious aniseed-like flavour. I would serve it in small portions, but if you want to make it a little lighter, don't use cashews. Fennel seeds are great for digestion and freshen the breath, usually chewed on in India after a meal, to counterbalance those heady masalas and their strong flavours.

Makes 2 glasses

4 tablespoons cashews
2 tablespoons chia seeds
2 teaspoons fennel powder or fennel seeds
1½ cups water
2 tablespoons almond butter
4–5 Medjool dates
a handful ice cubes, when blending

Soak the nuts and seeds for a couple of hours or overnight. Drain and mix with the fresh water, add the almond butter and dates and then blend together with the ice. If you don't have time to soak all the ingredients, at least try to soak the cashews for an hour.

Tip: If using fennel seeds, make sure you soak them with the mixture to ensure they blend well.

Simple Rose Falooda

Falooda is the ultimate Indian summer dessert or drink, typically made with various layers of milk, tukmaria or sabja seeds (similar to chia seeds), rose syrup, vermicelli or falooda sev (thin noodles), and topped with chopped nuts. You'll find this in many Indian restaurants and sometimes on the streets of India in the cities, but here's a simple version you can make at home; it's much less heavy and uses minimal ingredients – since the falooda sev isn't easy to find, I've omitted it in this recipe. In traditional Indian cookery we use sabja or tukmaria seeds in falooda, which are also called basil seeds. These are similar in texture and colour to chia seeds, so I've substituted chia here. In Ayurveda, sabja seeds are said to be very cooling for the body.

Serves 1

1–2 teaspoons chia seeds soaked in a few tablespoons of
     water beforehand – you can do this an hour before or
     the day before
1 cup of any milk you like
1–2 tablespoons rose syrup
a few ice cubes

Garnishes:
a handful chopped almonds and pistachios
rose petals (optional)

Optional addition:
top with a small scoop of vanilla ice cream

Mix together all the ingredients in a glass and stir well. If you want to create a layered drink so you can see the pink and white floating separately, pour the syrup first, then the soaked chia seeds, stir these together at the bottom of the glass, then add the ice cubes and pour over the milk. Don't stir this. Top with a scoop of ice cream, if using, and nuts and rose petals, and serve with a spoon.

Indian Lime Soda

Lime soda, or nimbu soda is a staple street-side drink in India: refreshing, cooling and, with the addition of black salt, great for digestion. This is the effervescent variation of nimbu pani, a lime water drink with salt or sugar sold practically everywhere, and the perfect thirst-quencher in the sweltering summer heat, helping to replenish the body with electrolytes lost through sweating. If you're visiting India, you should avoid drinking local water, so as tempting as the nimbu pani stalls look, with buckets of ice water and pyramids of limes set up on the cart, it's best to make your drink at home or order it in a hotel, where you can be sure it's made with bottled water. Mix the lime, sugar and salt first, before adding in the soda, as this will ensure the soda remains carbonated. You can also make this a salty nimbu soda, with no sugar, although the addition of sugar balances the flavours and gives it that distinctive khatta meetha (sweet-sour) flavour. This recipe traditionally has kala namak, or black salt, commonly used in Indian cuisine as a flavour enhancer. It has a sulphurous, pungent smell and is made by heating salt for several hours along with other spices, seeds and herbs. If you don't have black salt, as an alternative try the Ginger Lime Soda below. You can also use plain table salt, although this won't give you the sulphurous notes of black salt.

Makes 2 glasses

crushed ice or ice cubes
juice of 1 lime or lemon
¹/₅ teaspoon or a pinch of kala namak (black salt)
pinch of black pepper (optional)
2 teaspoons sugar or agave syrup
1 can soda water/330ml (around 1½ cups)

Optional garnishes:
mint leaves
slices of lemon or lime

Place the ice in a tall glass. Stir the lime juice, salt, pepper (if using) and sugar in a small mixing bowl until the salt and sugar completely dissolve. Add the lime juice mixture to the ice, slowly fill the glass almost to the top with soda water and stir briefly. Top with a last splash of soda, garnish with the mint leaves and lemon or lime slices, if using, and serve.

Ginger Lime Soda

This is great if you love a bit of a kick and spice. It's cooling, it's energising and you can also make it spicy and salty by omitting the sugar, if you like. I make a jar of the lime and ginger mixture and keep it in the fridge during summer, so that I can simply add water or soda to this whenever I feel like it. It keeps in the fridge for at least two weeks, as long as you don't add any water.

Makes 2 glasses

1 inch/2 cm piece ginger
juice of 1 lime or lemon
2 teaspoons sugar or agave syrup
¼ teaspoon ground cumin
pinch of ground black pepper (optional)
a few ice cubes (optional)
1 can soda water/330ml (around 1½ cups)

Optional garnishes:
mint leaves
slices of lemon or lime

To make the ginger juice, grate the ginger (you can keep the skin on) and squeeze the juice from the grated ginger with your fingers into the bowl. If a few ginger strands escape into the bowl, that's fine – great to chew on. You could also use a juicer, but I would only use this if making a larger quantity. You will get much more juice from the ginger by squeezing with your fingers and it's easy if it's a small amount.

Squeeze the lime into the bowl, add the sugar or agave, ground cumin and black pepper, and mix well. If using ice, then place ice in 2 tall glasses (I prefer not to use ice, as cold drinks are not recommended for health and digestion, according to Ayurveda). Add the lime and ginger juice mixture to the ice, slowly fill the glasses almost to the top with soda water and stir briefly. Top with an extra splash of soda, the mint leaves and lemon or lime slices, if using, and serve.

Orange, Coconut and Chilli Refresher

This is a deliciously refreshing drink with a kick and tropical vibes. A small piece of green chilli will boost the metabolism, the coconut milk makes it rich and frothy and there's a zesty sweetness from the orange.

Makes 2 glasses

1¼ cups coconut milk
2 clementines, seedless or seeds removed, peeled
¼ green chilli
2 tablespoons agave nectar (optional)
6–8 ice cubes

Blend everything in a high-speed blender for a few seconds until the ice is crushed and it's a smooth liquid. Strain into glasses. Alternatively, squeeze the juice from the oranges and blend this into the coconut milk, so that there are no bits, then you don't need to use a sieve.

Chai story: Chai by the Ganga

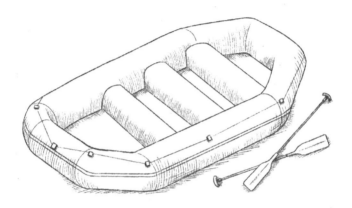

Maa Ganga, which literally translates as 'Mother Ganges', is considered India's most sacred river; and Rishikesh is the first city that Ganga flows through after descending the Himalayas. On the hour-long picturesque drive from Dehradun, the closest airport, to Rishikesh, you get a glimpse through the gaps between tall green trees of the rapid waters of the Ganga from high above. The holy city of Rishikesh, which rests in the foothills of the Himalayas, is known for its ashrams, or religious retreats, and yoga centres situated on both sides of the river, as well as the beautiful Ganga arti, a daily ceremonial ritual with music, prayer and a sea of moving candles.

Rishikesh is also associated with The Beatles and their sojourn to study transcendental meditation in 1968. You can still visit what is now known as the Beatles Ashram, but was in fact the ashram of Maharishi Mahesh Yogi, who taught transcendental

meditation to celebrities, where John Lennon and Paul McCart-
ney wrote over thirty songs, including most of the White Album.

It seems I had landed here in Rishikesh at just the perfect time.
It was the spring festival of Holi, when so many flock here from all
over India, as it is a national holiday, but Rishikesh is also spread
out and quiet, a spiritually charged place, a perfect location to
spend a religious festival. Holi is also a turn of the season, the
welcoming of the hotter months, and the climate here in the hills
is much cooler and just perfect at this time of year.

I'm here for a yoga retreat run by my friends Sunaina and
Mansi, and one of the activities planned for the retreaters is
white-water rafting, for which Rishikesh is well known. I'm the
opposite of an adrenalin junkie when it comes to sport, so I'm
scared, but this turns out to be the best and most exhilarating
experience of the entire trip. Equipped with our blue life vests, we
shuffle into a blue raft and float and splash through the various
rapids, tightly holding on to the handles on the raft. This is a section
of the river that is perfect for beginners, but there are also longer
four-hour and whole-day rafting experiences starting higher
up in the Ganga for professionals. The intense early-afternoon
heat dries us quickly as we flow through the calmer parts of the
river, only to get drenched again as we approach the next gushing
rapid. Midway through the journey, some of us jump into the cold,
fresh waters in a very calm area of the river – euphoric. And when
our jovial Nepalese guide asks us if we want to stop for maggi, the
instant curried noodles that are India's go-to two-minute meal,
we're ready! 'And chai,' calls my friend. We see a crowd of people on
the bank ahead of us and a number of red and blue rafts floating
in the water, while passengers eat and refuel.

We were, in fact, all waiting for this pitstop of hot noodles
and garam chai! Maggi noodles are the food of nostalgia you'll
find everywhere, from a child's lunchbox to the bubbling pans of

street vendors, who will serve it in hundreds of different ways. It's India's answer to the UK's Pot Noodle, and has achieved cult status here.

As the guide ties the raft to a rock with a sturdy rope, we remove our life vests and then help each other climb out of the raft. He passes us our phones from the bag he's kept safely tucked away, so we can take some photos in this spot, and we excitedly make our way up the rocks, dripping and drying, to where the noodles are being made. They're in a large pot, chai is on the boil too, and someone is selling snacks and water. Other groups are sitting dotted around, eating and posing for photographs. My friend places our order with a young man who is serving up the next batch of hot noodles while his friend pours milk into a large silver pan to make fresh chai. I climb a rock and step over a gap where the Ganga is rushing down the mountain, running over the rocks, so forceful it creates a pool of foam where it collects in an opening before trickling down the rest of the rocks to join the main river.

While we're posing for photographs, the men make their way to us and hand us our lunch, steaming curly noodles served on a silvery steel plate with a fork in a pool of brownish broth with the odd tiny green and orange vegetable, smelling so incredibly enticing, it doesn't matter that they don't look quite so enticing. And as expected, the noodles taste incredible; in fact, it's quite the five-star experience, surrounded only by water, rock and mountains. Chai soon follows – they take my plate, hand me a steel cup and pour steaming and perfectly brown milky chai from a large aluminium serving teapot, a black cloth loosely tied around the handle because the entire serving pot has been sitting on the stove to keep it hot. I'm now completely dry, the glaring sun on my back. I realise it is actually the perfect temperature – no wonder this is the season for Rishikesh. While temperatures are rising in the rest of India, the north is still warming up, with cooler evenings in the Himalayan foothills where Rishikesh is located.

We climb back onto our raft, hand over our phones and ride through the rest of the rapids with more ease, knowing what's coming. The final stop is near the famous Lakshman Jhula, a suspension bridge over the Ganga. Once upon a time this was a hanging jute structure, but it was transformed into an iron suspension bridge in 1930, connecting the east bank to the west bank of the river. Along with its counterpart Ram Jhula, these two bridges are landmarks of Rishikesh, with panoramic views of the riverbanks and city.

To think I was ready to miss this water-rafting part of the trip, and now I was ready to go again the next day. I'd been to Rishikesh twice when I was younger, but both were such fleeting trips that I didn't get a real flavour of it: the hippy cafés; Europeans and others wandering around, many on yoga teacher-training courses; tattoo shops, market stalls and shops selling holy mala bead chains, spiritual books, clothes, Tibetan bowls and more. And then, of course, the serene ashrams and resorts. It is peaceful yet bustling, a spiritual place I'll be returning to soon.

COOKING
WITH CHAI

I love infusing breakfast and dessert dishes with chai – the spices add a real depth of flavour to sweet recipes as well as warmth and nutritional benefits. The simple addition of cinnamon to porridge, for example, transforms the aroma and flavour into a rich and warming breakfast, perfect on colder mornings in the autumn and winter. According to Ayurveda, it is important to have foods that are warming in nature, and thus adding spices is one way of transforming the nature of food, enhancing its digestibility and maintaining our own agni (digestive fire). Chinese medicine also considers this important, describing warming foods as 'yang', likened to the warm, sunny side of a mountain, helping to raise the energy of the body by improving circulation and bringing heat to the organs, blood and cells.

You can experiment with spices and use different ones to create different flavours. Many Indian desserts are traditionally made with cardamom or saffron, for example, and I've included some of my favourites, from kheer (rice pudding) and gajar (carrot) halwa to the thick, sweet, saffron-spiced yoghurt called shrikhand. I've also added my own sweet creations that use chai spices, from a masala chai cake and banana crumble to spiced energy balls and chia puddings, covering breakfasts, desserts and sweet treats. With each dish, you have a plethora of garnishing options, which add texture, colour and make the dish look even more alluring – and you can use your own creative flair and add whatever you have in your kitchen. Lastly, I've focused on simplicity, ease and minimal ingredients, so you should find everything uncomplicated.

Breakfasts

Sweet Miso Chai Porridge

Salty miso with sweet maple syrup is a heavenly combination:
a satisfying umami flavour. Miso is a fermented paste made
from soybeans and grains that's been used in Japanese cuisine
for centuries and contains millions of gut-friendly bacteria that
help digestion.

Makes 1 large bowl or 2 small bowls

For the porridge:
4 tablespoons/40g oats
1 cup water
1 cup coconut milk (or any milk)
1 tablespoon flax or chia seeds (optional)

For the miso paste:
½ teaspoon miso paste
1 tablespoon honey
2 teaspoons almond butter or any nut butter
½ teaspoon cinnamon
¼ teaspoon cardamom
¼ teaspoon ginger

Optional toppings:
1–2 tablespoons coconut yoghurt
a handful pecan nuts, or any nuts or seeds you like
a sprinkle of coconut chips

Mix together all the ingredients for the sweet miso paste and keep ready in a small bowl. This paste will keep for 1–2 weeks in the fridge. To make the porridge, combine all the porridge ingredients in a pan and cook on a low to medium heat, stirring regularly. Once cooked, pour into a bowl and drizzle over the sweet miso paste, top with coconut yoghurt, pecan nuts and coconut chips, or any choice of toppings.

Saffron Chia Muesli

One of my favourite things to make in the summer is a soaked muesli: so simple and refreshing, and you can pretty much make it whatever flavour you like. It had to be saffron and cardamom for this particular recipe, however, echoing those summer colours, topped with colourful berries and pistachios. The chia seeds make it a little lighter than an exclusively oat mix.

Makes 1 large bowl or 2 small bowls

To soak:
4 tablespoons/40g oats
2 tablespoons chia seeds
¾ cup/200ml almond or coconut milk
1 apple, grated
1 teaspoon flax seeds
1 tablespoon pumpkin seeds
a pinch of saffron
½ teaspoon cardamom
2 tablespoons of honey (optional)
crushed walnuts (optional)

Optional toppings:
1–2 tablespoons yoghurt per bowl
a handful blueberries/raspberries
a sprinkle of pistachios

Combine all the muesli ingredients and stir well. Leave to soak for at least an hour, ideally a few hours or overnight. Taste for sweetness before serving, and you might need to add a little more milk. If you love a little extra crunch to your muesli, I'd recommend stirring in some broken walnuts. Top with the yoghurt, berries and pistachios, if using.

Orange and Cinnamon Muesli with Walnuts

Zesty orange with cinnamon is a winning and delicious combination. And if you squeeze the orange into the muesli with your hand, it's barely any extra fuss. Cinnamon adds sweetness and warmth, but you can add cardamom too if you like. Soaking oats overnight improves their nutritional benefits and makes them more digestible, so do try to make this the night before if possible.

Makes 1 large bowl or 2 small bowls

4 tablespoons oats
1 green apple, grated
1 teaspoon flax seeds
¾ cup/200ml almond or coconut milk
juice of half an orange
4 prunes, chopped
5 walnuts, broken
½ teaspoon cinnamon powder
ginger, a few very thin slices (optional)
2 teaspoons honey (optional)

Optional toppings:
a few mint leaves
a sprinkle of goji berries
extra cinnamon powder

Mix together all the ingredients for the muesli and soak for at least an hour, or in the fridge overnight. Your oats will absorb the liquid and swell over time when soaked, so although it may look very liquid at first, much of this will be absorbed by the morning. If you're in a rush, you can consume this within around half an hour of soaking, but the oats will not soak up all the liquid, so you might want to add a little less milk.

Cinnamon Sweet Potato with Nut Butter

My grandfather used to have mashed sweet-potato pudding, so I've taken that as inspiration and made this breakfast dish a little more decadent. I bake the sweet potato, mash it and then stir in maple syrup, cinnamon and cardamom, before adding a touch of oat or almond milk, and then stirring in some almond butter to make it even more delicious.

Serves 1

1 sweet potato (around 250g), peeled and roughly
   chopped
1 teaspoon cinnamon
¼ teaspoon cardamom
1 tablespoon almond or peanut butter
5 tablespoons milk
1 tablespoon honey or brown sugar

Serve with:
any yoghurt
granola
mixed nuts and seeds

Steam or boil the sweet potato until soft, combine with the rest of the ingredients, mash and mix together. Serve with a few tablespoons of your favourite yoghurt, a sprinkle of granola, or any nuts and seeds you like. This will keep in the fridge in an airtight container for 3–4 days.

Soaked Prunes with Chai Spices

This is a super-tasty and gut-friendly yoghurt, blended with prunes soaked in fragrant spices and tea. This is best made with plain yoghurt, with no added sugar. Prunes are a great source of fibre and thus aid digestion – they are well known to help relieve constipation and are also rich in antioxidants.

Serves 2 as part of a meal

10 prunes
½ cup/125ml water
2 cinnamon sticks
1 cardamom pod
2 cloves
1 star anise (optional)
plain yoghurt to serve

Optional toppings:
honey
granola

Simply soak the prunes in water with all the spices, leave overnight and serve the next day with yoghurt. You can also soak walnuts or any nuts with the prunes, if you like. Top with honey or granola to make it extra delicious.

Apple Crumble Baked Oats

Here's a healthy apple crumble breakfast or even something you can have for a wholesome dessert. It's warming, autumnal, deliciously spiced, and not too sweet. The combination of apples and cinnamon is heavenly, as ever. If you don't have almond flour, increase the quantity of oats and blitz them in a blender instead of using them whole.

Serves 2 as part of a meal

For the bake:
½ cup/40g oats
2 tablespoons almond flour
½ teaspoon baking powder
⅓ cup/80ml milk
1 teaspoon cinnamon
½ teaspoon cardamom
2 tablespoons maple syrup
1 small apple, cut into bite-size chunks
1 tablespoon raisins

Garnishes:
cinnamon powder
brown sugar

Serve with (optional):
soy yoghurt or coconut yoghurt
vanilla ice cream or custard

Preheat the oven to 190°C/375°F/gas mark 4. Mix all the ingredients together well, taste and make any adjustments. Pour this mixture into an ovenproof dish or two ramekins, sprinkle some cinnamon and brown sugar on top and place in the oven for 20–25 minutes. Serve hot with a cup of chai. You can also serve with a side of yoghurt or with vanilla ice cream for more of a dessert.

Chai, Fennel Seed and Coconut Granola

This granola was a winner at my café, Chai by Mira. It's such a delicious snack and goes well with cold milk, hot milk, yoghurt, berries or banana. This is one of my favourite takes on it, with the addition of fennel seeds giving it a hint of liquorice, plus lots of cinnamon and cardamom. I'd love you to experiment and come up with your own version.

Makes 6 servings

1¼ cup/150g oats
2 tablespoons/20g pumpkin seeds
1 tablespoooon/10g sunflower seeds
1 tablespoon/10g chopped almonds or nuts of your choice
½ cup/35g desiccated coconut
1 teaspoon/5–7g cinnamon
1 teaspoon/5–7g cardamom powder
2–3 tablespoons fennel seeds
a handful chopped dates, around 15g
a handful sultanas, around 15g
¼ cup/65g coconut oil
⅓ cup/75g honey or maple syrup

Preheat the oven to 190°C/350°F/gas mark 5. Mix together all the dry ingredients except for the dates and sultanas, then melt the coconut oil if not already liquid, and stir this and the honey or maple syrup into the dry mix. Taste and adjust as necessary, then spread the mixture on a baking tray and bake in the oven for around 25 minutes. Remove from the oven and stir the dates and sultanas into the mix – we add these in later to prevent them from going very hard, as it makes the granola difficult to chew and can break your teeth! – before returning to the oven for another 10 minutes. Remove from the oven, let it cool down and then transfer to an airtight jar, where it will keep for around three months.

Chai Oat Biscuits

These delicious biscuits are flavoured delicately with cinnamon and cardamom, lightly sweetened with maple syrup, and the perfect complement to a cup of coffee or simply dunked in milk. They're also a great way to add aromatic spices to your children's snacks.

Makes 10 biscuits

2 tablespoons/30g pecans and/or walnuts, toasted
2 tablespoons/20g oats
2 tablespoons/30g plain flour
2 tablespoons/25g coconut sugar or alternative
¼ teaspoon bicarbonate of soda
½ teaspoon cinnamon
½ teaspoon cardamom
2 tablespoons maple syrup
1 tablespoon coconut oil, melted
1 tablespoon milk
1 tablespoon ginger juice (optional)

Preheat the oven to 180°C/350°F/gas mark 4. Blitz the nuts and oats in a blender or food processer, and mix with the rest of the ingredients. Taste for sweetness and make any adjustment. Roll into small balls the size of a golf ball and flatten lightly using a fork, then place in the oven for 15–20 minutes. Leave to cool and then enjoy!

Banana Bread Overnight Oats

As you'll have worked out by now, I love different variations of overnight oats, with varying spices and different fruits. This one, made with lots of cinnamon and some banana, tastes rather like banana bread. Delicious to take on the go, especially as a post-workout snack. If you prefer apples, replace the banana with grated apple.

Serves 2

4–5 tablespoons/35g oats
1 tablespoon/10g flax seeds, whole or ground
1 teaspoon cinnamon powder
⅓ cup/80ml almond milk
1 tablespoon yoghurt
½ banana, around 50g, mashed
1 tablespoon maple syrup
1 tablespoon almond flour (optional)
a handful walnuts, broken (optional)

Mix together all the ingredients and leave overnight in the fridge. You can also eat this straightaway, but it does taste better if you leave it to soak for a little while.

Golden Spiced Blended Oats

In this recipe, I've blended the oats, which makes it easy to eat straightaway, rather than soaking overnight like overnight oats. However, you can also leave this in the fridge and have it the next day if you like. Adding turmeric and other spices makes this breakfast great for the gut, for immunity and much more. You can mix up the spices depending on what you have and what you like, so add, chop and change as you wish! And you can omit the honey entirely if you want to add pre-sweetened protein powder – I would recommend any vanilla protein powder.

Serves 1

50g/½ cup oats, blended in a high-speed blender into a
    coarse powder
⅓ cup/80ml almond milk, oat milk or coconut milk
2 teaspoons flax seeds
1 heaped teaspoon honey
½ teaspoon cinnamon
¼ teaspoon ginger
¼ teaspoon turmeric
3–4 prunes, chopped (or sultanas, both optional)
1 teaspoon peanut butter
2 tablespoons yoghurt, to serve

Garnish:
your favourite berries

Mix together all the ingredients except for the yoghurt. Taste and make any adjustments, in case you want more cinnamon or honey. Top with yoghurt and your favourite berries. You can also drizzle some peanut butter on top if you like.

Vanilla Chai Chia Pots

I love a chia pudding for breakfast or as a light sweet snack. Chia seeds feel lighter than oats so I often mix the two together; I love chia's gooey consistency once the seeds swell up, and they're very nutritious: 'One serving of 28 grams (g), or 2½ tablespoons, provides just under 10g of fibre. The daily recommendation for adults is 25–30g, so a serving of chia seeds can fulfill 30 per cent of this.'[*] Chia seeds are the richest plant source of omega-3 fatty acids, and are also a complete protein, containing all nine essential amino acids that cannot be made by the body.[†]

Here I've made a chia pudding or pot topped with almonds and pistachios. You can, of course, mix up the spices to your taste, and make it less or more sweet. To make it thicker and more rich, I've used thick coconut milk. It tastes divine!

2 tablespoons/20g chia seeds
½ cup coconut milk, from a tin
1 tablespoon maple syrup, agave syrup or honey
1 tablespoon vanilla essence
½ teaspoon cinnamon
¼ teaspoon cardamom

Garnish with:
2 tablespoons yoghurt
a drizzle of maple syrup or honey
chopped pistachios and almonds

---

* https://www.medicalnewstoday.com/articles/291334#nutrition
† https://www.hsph.harvard.edu/nutritionsource/food-features/chia-seeds/

Chai story: A miracle in Varanasi

Varanasi to Delhi, 2004

Varanasi, also known as Banaras and Kashi, was one of the places of pilgrimage that my grandparents visited on their eight-month yatra with their very young boys. Just as they reached Varanasi, a place my grandmother had desperately wanted to visit, and no sooner had they walked into the main Vishwanath temple area, than an accident happened. Their second child, my middle uncle, just four years old, was pushed aside by a rushing cow and hit his head on a large stone tulsi kyaro, a stone piece in which the sacred tulsi plant is kept. While my grandfather ran to find cotton wool or a bandage to stop the bleeding, my grandmother took her son outside the temple area and put him on her lap, blood dripping on her sari. A man, as Bhabhi has told me several times over the years, came and placed a white cloth on my uncle's head. She saw his feet and knew that he was wearing saffron clothes, but was focused on her son and thus didn't look up. The bleeding sud-

denly stopped, but when she glanced up to thank him, the man had disappeared. Babhai, my grandfather, arrived soon after and Bhabhi relayed this story. He went looking for this man but found him nowhere. Bhabhi is certain he was Shankar Bhagwan, she says – God himself, who saved her son.

It was the very same Varanasi that I was now visiting, many years later in December 2004, a sacrosanct place from a bygone era that seems never to change. The 2,525-kilometre-long Ganga, known as 'Ganga ma' or Mother Ganges, most sacred of rivers and considered a living goddess, flows through the city. Hindus believe that bathing in her waters can cleanse a person of a lifetime of sins, and that to die and be cremated in Varanasi helps achieve moksha (salvation), a release from the continuous cycle of life, death and rebirth, and this is why many travel to this city as they approach the last days of their life. A soul-stirring, mystical place, Varanasi stands still in time, immersed in orange hues and the golden light from the huge flames of the cremations and the diyas of the aarti ceremonies. It is spiritually charged, infinitely peaceful, a profound reminder of the circle of life and the ritual of death – indeed, somewhere the veil between life and death seems very thin. In Mark Twain's words, 'I think Banaras [Varanasi] is one of the most wonderful places I have ever seen. It has struck me that a Westerner feels in Banaras very much as an oriental must feel while he is planted down in the middle of London.'

I had been there for a spiritual festival, staying on one of the ghaats (embankments) of the Ganga for over a week, surrounded by ritualistic cremations and pujas, wooden riverboats floating past, men and sari-clad women bathing, immersing themselves head to toe or pouring the holy Ganga water over themselves with a cup, heavenly chants and sounds resonating through the air.

Finally, it had come time to leave, and, travelling alone, I needed to reach Delhi to continue my onward journey. The local *travel agency told me that the only feasible option was to take a train from a station on the Bihar border, but that it was a very large station where it could be difficult to find the right train. That train was also scheduled to leave in the middle of the night, and the car journey to Bihar too a few hours. Seeing I was a little worried, the owner of the agency offered to take me himself. The roads were bumpy and dark, and at one point I felt like I was going through a forest: I was sitting in the back of a small car, squashed beside my trolley bag, leaning on it, falling asleep. Somehow I had almost lost my voice and was barely audible to my father, who was calling me on my metallic-blue Nokia phone, which was about to die. I was repeating mantras in my mind, praying that my instinct to trust this driver was right. This was possibly the most potentially dangerous situation I'd ever been in.*

Eventually, when we reached our destination, my driver offered to check on the train – and it was apparently two hours delayed. He said it wasn't safe to wait alone at this station, that it was very easy to get on the wrong train and so he would wait with me in the car. Eventually I fell asleep, only to find him waking me up at the right time. He dropped me at the correct carriage – first class – put my bags inside and left. A miracle, I thought to myself, just as my grandmother did all those years ago, as I gratefully said goodbye. Anything could have gone wrong, and yet here I was in the right place, on my way to Delhi. The train swiftly left, so I got under the blanket in the cold air-conditioned cabin and fell asleep.

When I woke up a few hours later it was early morning, and a couple in their sixties was sitting upright in the top bed opposite me, having a morning chai as we stood still at the penultimate station to Delhi. They had been asleep when I entered the cabin last night.

We started speaking in English – they were from Delhi, seemed very well-to-do, on their way back from a short holiday and pilgrimage. I looked outside at the relatively quiet platform, looking for the chaiwala. 'Would you like some?' the lady asked, passing me her Haldiram's crispy sev-and-nut snack. (Haldiram is one of the most famous Indian brands for namkeen, savoury snacks, as well as sweets.) I was a little more audible this morning, but my throat was still sore, and the air-conditioning in the train cabin hadn't helped. But at least the fear I had last night, travelling with a man I hardly knew, who of course had turned out to be some sort of guardian angel, was now gone. I could relax. I was safe. The young boy with a metal flask of chai was coming my way. I walked out to the door of the carriage, happy to get some fresh air. I took the paper cup from the boy and waited for him to fill it with the very well-brewed brown liquid – not too milky, I was happy to find.

Snacks

Saffron Oat and Coconut Biscuits

I love the subtlety of saffron, a gentle yet fragrant and delicious spice – so much so that I called my first book *Saffron Soul*. I also just love the combination of blended oats and coconut, so that you almost can't tell there's any coconut in there. These are light and oaty biscuits, made wonderfully rich by the saffron strands.

Makes around 15 biscuits

1 cup/100g oats
½ cup/50g flaked coconut
¼ cup/20ml coconut oil
5 tablespoons water
2–3 tablespooons sugar, maple syrup or agave
¼ teaspoon saffron strands

Preheat the oven to 180°C/350°F/gas mark 4. Combine the oats and coconut in a blender and blend until you have a floury powder. Now mix with the rest of the ingredients and roll out into a dough. Using a cookie cutter or the rim of a small glass, cut out round biscuits. Grease your baking tray, place on the tray and put into the oven for 15–18 minutes. Let the biscuits cool before eating or placing in a jar.

Ginger Peanut Butter Cookies

These warming, nutty and gingery biscuits taste of autumn. Of course, you can add any spices you like and even make these without spices, but I do love ginger biscuits, so that's the flavour I was trying to get; and cardamom pairs deliciously with ginger.

Makes 9–12 cookies

½ cup/50g oats
1 cup/100g smooth peanut butter
3 tablespoons/40g coconut sugar or any sugar
1 teaspoon ginger powder
¾ teaspoon cardamom powder

Preheat over to 180°C/350°F/gas mark 4. Blend the oats in a high-speed blender until they have the consistency of flour. If there are some larger oat flakes, this is fine. Mix together all the ingredients. The consistency should be sticky but firm so you can form balls. If it's too dry (this might be because your peanut butter was more solid than runny), then add 2 teaspoons or more of coconut oil. Add just a little, then increase if you need to. Shape into 9–12 golf-ball-sized balls and flatten slightly (you can use a fork to press down gently). Place on a greased baking tray and cook in the preheated oven for 20 minutes. Let them cool and then dunk into your coffee or chai.

Cocoa Cinnamon Energy Balls

I love nibbling on an energy ball. The ones I make for myself are small and manageable, but you can make them whatever size you want. You can make a batch and store them in the fridge for weeks, or you can even serve them up at the end of a dinner party, jazzed up with a drizzle of melted chocolate, some chopped berries or even mint leaves. They're also great as kids' lunchbox snacks (provided where your kids are going allows nuts) and rather fun to make with kids too – much less messy than baking!

Makes around 10 balls

½ cup/50g oats
¼ cup/75g peanut or almond butter
3 tablespoons honey
1 tablespoon cocoa powder
½ teaspoon cinnamon powder
¼ teaspoon ginger powder (optional, for an extra kick)
1–2 tablespoons desiccated coconut to roll the balls in
(optional)

Stir together all the ingredients except the coconut, roll into small balls, then roll each ball in the coconut and place in the fridge. They'll keep for at least 2 weeks.

Christmas Spice Energy Balls

Star anise powder, also called Badian powder, is a fine dark brown powder with a sweet and fragrant liquorice aroma. These oat and peanut butter energy balls contain star anise powder, but you can add other spices if you like. Studies have shown that star anise can help treat depression and is rich in iron. Covering the energy balls in dark chocolate is an optional addition.

Makes around 10–15 balls

¾ cup/70g oats
½ cup/50g almond flour
2 tablespoons coconut oil, melted
1 heaped teaspoon anise powder
1 tablespoon peanut butter
1 tablespoon honey

Optional additions:
1 teaspoon of cinnamon and ¼ teaspoon ginger powder to
    make it more spicy
2 tablespoons dark chocolate chips and ½ teaspoon of
    coconut oil

Combine the oats, almond flour, coconut oil, anise powder, peanut butter and honey. Taste and make any adjustments, and add the optional spices if you would like them. Roll into balls (around 12–15g depending on the size you like). Place the balls in the fridge to solidify for around 1 hour or overnight. If you're covering them in chocolate, then combine the dark chocolate chips with ½ teaspoon of coconut oil in a small bowl, then immerse the bottom half of this bowl in a pan of boiling water, so that no water can fall into the bowl. Leave this to melt on a low heat for a few minutes or until the chocolate is melted. Remove from heat and stir the dark chocolate and coconut oil together. Now dip the balls in the melted chocolate, and place them back in the fridge so that the chocolate sets.

Chai story: A monsoon chai

Mumbai, 2012

There I was, thinking the Mumbai monsoons hadn't been too bad this time. But the one day I needed to shop, wanted to do a yoga class and move around, there was such an intense and heavy downpour I contemplated spending the entire day in my hotel. Lovely as the surroundings were, though, working on my laptop or using the spa did not appeal today, in this electric city I so love, and on what happened to be one of my last days in India on this trip.

Breakfast, as in every hotel in Mumbai, had been sumptuous, with overwhelming choice and a large pot of well-boiled ginger-spiced chai made with the requested soya milk. Drinking a small shot glass of chai with cow's milk on the street feels fine on the stomach, but a larger quantity with rich, heavy milk is too much to digest for me. Today the chai had been served with a plain dosa, one of my favourite South Indian breakfast dishes, a thin savoury pancake made with lentils and rice, served with coconut chutney, green coriander chutney and spicy tomato chutney. This is usually also served with a mashed masala potato mixture stuffed inside the dosa, but you can also have it plain – if a potato curry for breakfast doesn't quite appeal. A meal in itself, it was freshly made at an open counter where the chef was using every inch of his large tava (griddle), enough to make five oval dosas at once.

Grey and gloomy outside, it felt like one of those London mornings when I just do not want to shift from my bed, but this was India. Mumbai, always on the move, was calling me into her streets, calling me to see the day plod along, not troubled by the greys, flooding waters or crazy traffic. It turned out that by the time I left an hour later, having had a half-hour head massage (one of the joys of being in India), the rain had calmed down, but the generous drops still landed on my hair as I ducked into the black-and-yellow auto-rickshaw outside the hotel, with navy seats that looked new and walls painted with the faces of Bollywood stars from the nineties. The smell of rain, of the earth and leaves, filled the air.

Seeing Mumbai while sitting in a rickshaw is always more interesting, more open, more connected to life outside, and you feel more alive to all the senses than in a car, but the season made it all the more fascinating. I could hear the sound of pattering rain, of incessant horns, of the engine of my rickshaw, merged into one, and all the while water was spraying on my face as we drove smoothly along the roads. We stopped in a traffic jam, sandwiched between the backs and fronts and sides of so many vehicles. A man holding his umbrella ran in front of us. There was a line of water streaming onto the street from the side of a *bus nearby. A lady wearing a sari walked with her feet immersed deep inside a seemingly endless puddle. I turned to watch the life of a few families living under the bridge beside me and saw a mother lay her baby on a rock as she tended to her other children. The disparity of wealth is so palpable and stark in a city like Mumbai, the most densely packed city on earth, but there is also a sense of joy, survival and life on every street and every street corner.*

We approached Linking Road, also known as Link Road, a famous shopping road in Bandra, with shoe and clothes shops on one side and stalls selling shoes, accessories, belts, cosmetics and clothes on the other, and just then, stopping at a traffic light, the gentle pitter-patter of rain developed into the sound of drums as it fell on the roof above me. The shops on my right, one after another, that famously line this whole stretch of road, were cocooned from the surge of water, but on the other side, stall after stall brimming with bags and shoes was semi-exposed, the stallholders trying to shield their goods and move them under cover.

Linking Road, at the centre of everything, is a prominent arterial road connecting Bandra, Khar and Santacruz, and is one you will most likely pass each time you come to this city to go from one area to another. Years ago, as children, we loved shopping here with my mum, but as the shopping in Mumbai developed and our tastes changed, the shopping on this road came to seem ancient – it's wonderful to get a good bargain, but you also compromise on quality. Each time I pass Link Road, though, it brings back memories of my childhood trips to Mumbai. Little did I know then that in my twenties I would end up spending weeks and months in Bandra, an area which has become the most cosmopolitan in the city, that I would be working from here, having a life here, making friends in Mumbai. Bandra is filled with expats and young Bombayites, brimming with cafés, *restaurants and bars, and feels like it's in the heart of the city, as this is also where the Sea Link is, the bridge connecting north to south Mumbai.*

Mumbai might be notorious for traffic, for severe rains in the monsoon, for pollution, there might be muddy potholes and puddles everywhere, but there's something enticing about the city at this time of year.

After a yoga class at Yoga House, which had become one of my favourite yoga studios in my late twenties, and having stopped by Anokhi, a shop I can't miss on any trip to India, known for reviving Rajasthani block printing, I met my friend Sunaina for chai and pakora at a tiny dhaba-style restaurant called Papa Pancho in Pali Hill, the heart of Bandra. I've only ever had their tadka daal in the past, but this was an early-evening monsoon-special treat, chai and pakora, a pairing that Indians always find comforting during the monsoons. The rain seemed to have finally stopped, the air was damp with warmth, and my clothes, dampened in the earlier downpours, were almost dry.

We ordered the aloo (potato) and onion pakora, long slices of both, dipped in a gram-flour batter and fried until they're brown and crisp. The chai arrived piping hot, less sweet, as requested. We had pakora, or what we called bhajias in Gujarati growing up – my grandmother would fry potato bhajias, onion bhajias, even ones with banana slices. Now and again, she made these fresh for my grandfather as a lunch. He loved onion bhajias, potato bhajias and methi (fenugreek) bhajias, made with fresh methi leaves, or what we call 'methi na gota', always hot and fresh.

---

* 'Bombay' and 'Mumbai' are used interchangeably and so are 'Bombayites' and 'Mumbaikars', sometimes depending on which language is being spoken or what the Bombayite associates with.

I hadn't grown up knowing this pairing of bhajias and chai, nor had I ever loved the combination particularly, but sitting here having them dipped in mint chutney while slurping garam chai as the skies darkened and evening approached, it seemed like the perfect antidote to the rains and grey skies.

I hadn't been here for the first rain – even now, people go out to get drenched in the first rain of the monsoon – but as I stood on the corner of a street in Bandra, waiting for a rickshaw to stop for me after dinner, I found myself walking further and savouring the rain, enjoying the puddles and getting wet.

Desserts

Shrikhand

This has to be one of my favourite thali treats, saved for a special occasion or when we have guests. Shrikhand is a creamy, sweet and saffron-spiced yoghurt traditionally made with home-made strained or hung yoghurt, although these days I make it with the thickest Greek yoghurt I can find. I remember my grandmother tying up the yoghurt in a muslin cloth and leaving the water to drain in a pan, with the top of the muslin cloth hanging over the edge, held together by a steel plate. The luxuriously creamy yoghurt is whisked with sugar, saffron and cardamom, then topped with sliced almonds, pistachios and sometimes with rich red pomegranate seeds.

Serves 4–6

2 cups/500g thick Greek yoghurt
6–8 tablespoons sugar or honey
½ teaspoon cardamom powder
¼ teaspoon saffron strands
1 tablespoon almonds and pistachios, finely chopped,
    for garnishing
1 tablespoon pomegranate seeds for garnishing (optional)

Place the yoghurt in a mixing bowl and add the sugar or honey, cardamom powder and saffron. Stir thoroughly so that the colour of the saffron strands beautifully laces the yoghurt. Taste and make any adjustments. Place in a serving bowl and garnish with pistachios, almonds and pomegranate seeds if you have them.

Carrot Cake Masala Chai Cupcakes

Fluffy and moist, lightly sweet and subtly spiced, these make for a deliciously healthy treat for all ages, and a great lunchbox or snack treat. Adding spices to baked dishes and food brings flavour and an abundance of health benefits. They're also super-easy to make and need no fancy equipment – simply stirring with a spoon. If you love a nutty crunch in your cakes, add nuts inside the batter as well as the suggested garnishing.

Makes 8 cupcakes

Tea mix:
½ cup of any milk you like
1 teabag (or 2 if you want it stronger) or
    1 teaspoon tea leaves
½ teaspoon cinnamon
½ teaspoon cardamom
½ teaspoon ginger
¼ teaspoon nutmeg

Cupcake mixture:
1 cup/100g plain flour
⅓ cup/50g olive oil
¼ teaspoon baking powder
¼ teaspoon bicarbonate of soda
3 tablespoons/35g soft brown sugar
1 small carrot, grated

Garnishes:
a handful walnuts, broken
cinnamon to sprinkle on top

Preheat the oven to 190°C/375°F/gas mark 5. Boil together the milk with the tea and spices for 5–10 minutes on a low to medium heat. In the meantime, mix together the flour, oil, baking powder, bicarbonate of soda and sugar, then add the grated carrot and the boiled liquid mixture.

Mix this well, taste and make any adjustments. Brush cup-cake holders with oil, spoon in the batter, filling the cups to halfway. Garnish with broken walnuts or any other nuts or seeds, if you like, as well as a sprinkle of cinnamon.

Bake for 20 minutes, leave to cool, then serve with a cup of chai.

Masala Chai Cake

I love spices in cakes – well, in everything! And here's a moist and delicious eggless cake recipe infused with chai spices, topped with a mix of coarsely ground cardamom and brown sugar – divine! It's incredibly easy to make, the yoghurt works in place of an egg and I've added a touch of tea.

Makes 1 cake

1 cup/245g yoghurt
½ teaspoon bicarbonate of soda
¾ cup/150g brown sugar
⅓ cup/70g ghee or melted butter
½ cup/120g milk
1 teaspoon baking powder
1½ cups/220g plain flour
1½ teaspoon ground cinnamon
1 teaspoon ground cardamom (plus some more
    to sprinkle on top)
1 teaspoon ground ginger

Tea mix:
1 teaspoon black tea
small amount of water, around 2 tablespoons/30ml

Preheat the oven to 180°C/350°F/gas mark 4. Mix together the yoghurt and bicarbonate of soda, then stir in the sugar, ghee or melted butter and milk. Now add the baking powder and the flour into the mix, and lastly stir in all the spices. Boil the tea in a small amount of water, sieve the tea and stir this in. You can whisk the batter if you like, but it works fine if you thoroughly mix it with a spoon. Lightly sprinkle the top of the cake with extra cardamom and brown sugar. Transfer into a cake tin and bake for 40–45 minutes. To check it's baked, pierce with a fork and see that it comes out clean. Enjoy!

Tip: You can also use my Chai by Mira classic chai spice for this recipe. If using, swap this for the sugar, so ¾ cup/150g classic chai spice in place of brown sugar. Taste the batter and add a little more spice if you want to, otherwise top the cake with extra cardamom and sugar if you can.

Banana Cinnamon Crumble

I've always loved crumble – any kind of crumble. Here's a naturally sweeter one, as it's made with ripe bananas, and it therefore doesn't need lots of extra sugar. This is incredibly comforting, like a big hug with a big dose of cinnamon. The cinnamon in this, of which I've added a lot, adds even more sweetness, depth and warmth. Do make sure the banana is ripe – the riper the better, so it's sweeter and also soft. If the banana skin is blackening, that's perfect! This might mean it's quite mushy inside, which is fine, but just be careful when mixing it with the spices and sugar. And if you don't have or don't like nutmeg, just use cinnamon instead. You can also substitute plain or wholewheat flour for the almond flour.

Serves 2

For the filling:
2 small, ripe bananas, cut into chunks about an inch wide
1½ teaspoons cinnamon
¼ teaspoon nutmeg
1 tablespoon brown sugar or maple syrup

For the crumble:
3 tablespoons oats
3 tablespoons almond flour
1 tablespoon room temperature or cold butter
1 tablespoon brown sugar
a pinch of salt
a handful broken walnuts or pecans

Serve with:
custard or ice cream (optional)

Heat the oven to 190°C/375°F/gas mark 5. Mix the banana slices with the cinnamon, nutmeg and sugar or maple syrup in a mixing bowl. Transfer into a baking dish and flatten a little. Now mix together the oats, almond flour, butter, sugar and salt, rubbing it with your fingertips so that the mixture looks like moist breadcrumbs. Pour the crumb mix over the bananas and spread evenly using a fork. Sprinkle the nuts, a little more cinnamon and brown sugar on top. Bake in the oven for 20–25 minutes, let it cool or serve immediately with custard, ice cream or even by itself. It tastes great with a cup of spiced coffee.

Spiced Apple Crumble Cake

If you like cake, crumble and chai spices, this is a winner. It's made in two parts and is actually much simpler than you think. This is the creation of my talented colleague, Sara Jagnani, who started off working in my café and now has her own baking company. Sara makes some of the most deliciously spiced cakes I've ever tried. The crumble adds a wonderful crunch to the smooth texture of the cake. Lightly spiced, crunchy and moist – full of delicious contrasts. The almond flour adds a wonderful nuttiness to the crumble mixture, but if you don't have almond flour, please use an extra 20g of plain or oat flour.

Serves 2

For the crumble topping:
¼ cup/60g soft butter (not melted)
2 tablespoons/20g brown sugar
2 tablespoons/20g granulated sugar
½ cup/75g plain flour or oat flour
2½ tablespoons/20g almond flour
½ teaspoon baking powder
½ teaspoon cinnamon powder
½ teaspoon ginger powder
½ teaspoon vanilla

For the cake batter:
¼ cup/60g melted butter
⅓ cup/75g yoghurt
¾ cup/150g sugar
1 peeled and diced green apple, finely chopped

1¼ cups/150g plain flour

1 teaspoon/5g bicarbonate of soda

1 teaspoon cinnamon

1 teaspoon ginger powder

¼ teaspoon cardamom powder

¼ teaspoon pepper

4–6 tablespoons milk (as necessary if the batter is
  too thick)

Preheat your oven to 180°C/350°F/gas mark 4 and line a 7-inch (20cm) cake tin with greaseproof paper.

For the crumble: Mix the butter and sugars together in a mixing bowl. Add the rest of the crumble ingredients and whisk until combined. The consistency should be crumbly. Keep aside.

For the cake: In a bowl, mix together the melted butter, yoghurt and sugar until the sugar is fully dissolved. Add the chopped apple and the rest of the ingredients and mix well.

Pour the cake batter into the baking tin and top it with the cake crumble, then bake for 20–25 minutes or until a fork comes out clean. Don't overbake, or the crumble might get too hard. Transfer to a wire rack to cool. Sprinkle with some chai spice mix or cinnamon and enjoy.

Parle-G and Coconut Cheesecake

There had to be one Parle-G creation in this book, because this biscuit that has become a symbol in India of both consumer citizenship and of home. It's a staple in villages, in metros, on roadside highways, supermarkets and now internationally, nostalgic and transcending generations (see page 222 for more on Parle-G). So, here's a decadent dessert with crunchy Parle-G biscuit layers. This gets even better after some time in the fridge, and is a perfect make-ahead dessert.

Serves 4–6 in serving glasses

1 cup/250ml water
1–2 teaspoons instant coffee or 2 espresso shots
½ teaspoon cinnamon
¼ teaspoon ginger
¼ teaspoon cardamom powder
⅛ teaspoon nutmeg
⅔ cup/150ml double cream
¼ cup/40g caster sugar
½ cup/125g mascarpone cheese or cream cheese
    (at room temperature)
80g (1 pack) of Parle-G biscuits
cocoa powder for dusting

Boil the water and coffee with the spices. Meanwhile, beat the double cream and caster sugar with a whisk, add the mascarpone or cream cheese and continue to whip. Dip one Parle-G biscuit at a time in the coffee, and then place to make a layer in each of the glasses.

Spread a thick layer of the whipped cream mixture on top of the first layer of biscuits. Repeat process with the second layer of biscuits and cream mixture.

Dust the top with cocoa powder, using a sieve if desired. Refrigerate for about 2–4 hours before serving.

Kheer – Saffron Rice Pudding

Kheer is a quintessentially Indian sweet dish, a rice pudding made with milk and rice, spiced with cardamom, saffron, nutmeg and mixed nuts. It is made all over the subcontinent, especially for festivals and celebrations. It is believed that the first ever kheer was made at the Lord Jagannath temple at Puri, Odisha, about 2,000 years ago, and thus kheer is made during Hindu rituals at temples and in homes to this day and distributed to devotees as prashad, food that is offered to the Gods and deities first. However, it makes for a comforting and rich dessert anytime! Some like to add condensed milk to add sweetness and richness; in some parts of India, it is sweetened with jaggery; and many also like to add cashews and raisins. Kheer is also known by different names in different regions of India: payasam in Tamil, payesh in Bengali and ksheeram in Sanskrit. Here's how we have always made it at home, during pujas or religious ceremonies or simply as a delicious dessert served with a thali meal, a perfect accompaniment to roti.

Serves 4–6

For the rice:
¾ cup/150g basmati rice
2 cups/500ml water

For the milk:
½ cup/120g sugar
½ teaspoon nutmeg
1 teaspoon cardamom
¼ teaspoon saffron strands

3 cups/700ml whole milk
3 tablespoons almonds and pistachios, chopped,
    plus extra to garnish

Wash the rice 4–5 times under cold running water to remove the starch, then cover with fresh water and boil on a low to medium heat in a large pan until very soft (so you can add the milk later). This will take around 15–20 minutes. Using your spoon, mash the rice lightly so it becomes mushy. Now mix all the spices and sugar into the cold milk, pour this into the mushed rice and keep stirring, still on a low to medium heat. Add the nuts, stir well and let the kheer cook for 10–15 minutes until the mixture thickens. When serving, garnish with more chopped pistachios and almonds. If you're serving later, the kheer will thicken, so you can add a little more milk to achieve the consistency you want.

Tip: You can use plant-based milk for this, but ideally a thicker milk, such as oat milk or coconut milk, so that the dessert is creamy. And if you want the colour of the kheer to be a little yellow from the saffron, as it traditionally is, please use white sugar, or, alternatively, you can use agave. Brown sugar or coconut sugar are also great to use, but this may mean the dessert is a light brown colour.

Chai Fudge

This chickpea flour and date mixture has a fudge-like texture and is my own plant-based version of a traditional Indian sweet called monhanthal. I've used dates rather than sugar here, which gives a wonderful crunchy texture and a caramel-like sweetness. The chickpea flour is slightly nutty, and the warming spices make it even more aromatic. I've made this for years for my events and my café using only cardamom, but you can use other spices too, which is why I've called this version chai fudge.

Makes 20–25 pieces

⅓ cup/80ml coconut oil
1 cup/100g chickpea (gram) flour
4–5 dates (roughly ½ cup/100g), stones removed
1 teaspoon cardamom
½ teaspoon cinnamon
½ teaspoon ginger
¼ teaspoon nutmeg

Topping:
sliced almonds and pistachios
dark chocolate, melted (optional)

Start by melting the coconut oil in a large pan, then pour in the chickpea flour and stir on a low heat. While stirring, warm the dates in the microwave for 30 seconds or until soft so that they will melt easily when added to the chickpea flour and coconut oil mixture. Keep stirring the chickpea flour mixture for around 12–15 minutes until the mixture starts to thicken and you notice the colour change very slightly from yellow to orange/light brown. Now take the pan off the heat as you add in the warmed dates and stir them vigorously until they melt. The mixture does not need to be entirely smooth – the dates will add a lovely crunchy texture. Add the rest of the ingredients, whichever spices you like. Lay the mixture in a 7-inch × 7-inch (20cm × 20cm) baking tray and flatten using a palette knife or the back of a flat spoon, then sprinkle over the nuts and flatten again. If adding melted dark chocolate, pour it over evenly.

Transfer the baking tray to the fridge overnight. Remove it from the fridge for half an hour so that it softens before cutting into around 25 pieces. Store these in an airtight container in a cool place. The fudge will keep for 3–4 weeks. Serve in small glasses or bowls, topped with melted chocolate and nuts or ice cream or even berries.

Gajar Halwa

This popular Indian dessert is made from grated carrots, cooked in milk and sugar, spiced with cardamom and garnished with nuts. It comes from North India, where the winter months are the season for beautiful red carrots. These are naturally sweeter and thus perfect for a dessert, and give the halwa a vibrant colour. There are various ways of making gajar halwa, but here's the way my mum has taught me.

Serves 4

1 tablespoon ghee or oil
4 carrots (around 300g), peeled and grated
½ cup/125ml thick milk, e.g. whole milk, oat or
    coconut milk
4 tablespoons brown sugar
a pinch saffron
¾ teaspoon cardamom powder
a handful cashews, soaked for an hour or overnight
    (optional)
1 tablespoon chopped almonds and pistachios,
    for garnishing
1 scoop vanilla ice cream or coconut ice cream

In a pan, heat the ghee or oil, add the grated carrots and stir. Let this cook for 5–7 minutes on a low heat, stirring regularly. Now add the milk and keep stirring on a low to medium heat until the milk has fully soaked into the carrots (around 10 minutes). The sugar, saffron, cardamom and cashews can be added in now. Mix well and let this cook for a further 10 minutes, stirring regularly. Place into serving bowls hot, garnish with a sprinkle of almonds and pistachios, and add a scoop of ice cream to each bowl.

CHAI
ACCOMPANIMENTS

Traditionally, a cup of masala chai is as sweet as it is strong and spicy, and thus it goes well with savoury dishes, often with some spice such as deep-fried marchas (whole green chillies). Sunday mornings in Gujarat, the state of India where my family is from, start with chai and freshly fried ganthia (chickpea flour fried crackers, of which there's a whole variety) and jalebi (spiral-shaped crisp and juicy sticky sweet things), as well as a side of beautifully blistered whole marcha – whether you're in the city of Ahmedabad or a remote village, you'll find this or something similar, with a cup of garam (hot) and meethi (sweet) chai, of course.

Shops in the Indian – or rather very Gujarati – areas of London such as Wembley, serve up fresh ganthia, jalebi, marcha and dhokla on Sunday mornings too, and are always sold out by midday. Even though we kids have grown up eating porridge and having sweeter dishes for breakfast, my parents still have to end their breakfast on a savoury note, so even if they start with porridge, they need a bite of khakhra or ganthia with their cup of chai to end the meal. The chai is incomplete without a savoury something.

Thepla are another typically Gujarati breakfast or any time of day dish, almost synonymous with being Gujarati – something I ate for weekend breakfasts growing up. These wheat spiced rotis are something all Gujaratis take wrapped up in tin foil when they're travelling as thepla last for days and provide a Gujju fix with hot chai (again Gujaratis carry their masala powder, which they can magically sprinkle into a cup of English tea). Thepla are usually made with enough oil to make sure they keep well (so basically as good as deep-fried), but if you're having one fresh and hot off the stove, which makes it truly irresistible, you would tear it with your fingers like a roti, dip it in athanu or pickles – my favourite is gor keri (see page 95 for my nani's gor keri recipe) and even take a bite of deep-fried marchu or green chilli with each bite of thepla (or theplu – the singular form of the word). And lastly, even though yoghurt and chai aren't the best of combinations, I rather love a theplu dipped in home-made curd or yoghurt too!

Something equally popular in the north of India, in Punjab, is aloo paratha, a flaky flatbread or roti filled with a spiced mashed potato stuffing ('aloo' means potato). Parathas are also sometimes made with a cauliflower and cabbage stuffing, or even with paneer, served with some pickle or yoghurt to cool the spice, and indeed a cup of chai, especially if it's for breakfast. Aloo paratha, while it is typically a Punjabi dish, is something you'll find all over India.

As you will see in my story on page 270, chai and pakoras (which we call bhajia in Gujarati) is another delightful pairing, especially in the Indian monsoons. These fried, light and crispy spiced fritters made of vegetables, dipped in a chickpea flour and spice batter, are something that Indians crave as soon as the rains start in July. You'll find this combination everywhere on the streets, at stalls and in restaurants, and there are plenty of variations, from the traditional onion pakora and palak (spinach) pakora to aloo pakora, paneer pakora, gobhi pakora and moong dal pakora. I've given the easier-to-make, pan-fried versions of these fritters in this chapter.

Another popular Mumbai ritual is chai with bun maska, a slightly sweet white bun, cloud-like in its softness, laden with dollops of maska (whipped butter and cream) and served with kadka chai. The ritual of bun maska and chai involves dipping the bun into the hot tea and mopping up every last drop of the chai with the bun. Brun maska is similar but the bun is crusty instead of smooth. You'll find this particularly in the Irani cafés (see page 100).

Another typical Indian breakfast pairing is a slice of simple milky-white-looking bread, ideally from an unsliced loaf so you can cut yourself a thick wedge, toasted on a mesh over a naked flame, so it gets those lovely char marks, then slathered in butter. Pour yourself a cup of overboiled masala chai, brewed with whichever spices you like, and dunk away. As you bite into it, you taste the luxuriously soggy concoction of butter, soft bread and sweet milky chai; and bite after bite, you keep slurping on chai, balancing the act of slowly savouring and drinking while the chai is still hot hot hot.

Just as popular in Mumbai is the masala omelette and egg bhurji. I've given recipes for this desi omelette and for tofu bhurji, as a variation of the egg bhurji, in this chapter. Then there's the vegetable cutlet, also known as tikki, a popular Indian roadside food. The word 'cutlet' actually comes from the French word côtelette, first known to be used in 1682. Crisp on the outside and soft on the inside, this is a great teatime snack. There are many different versions of the cutlet, whose invention dates back to colonial times, when the British came to Bengal and Lord Amherst started the cultivation of potatoes there, one of the first things he did as Governor-General in 1823. The colonial cooks would mash boiled potatoes and mix them with minced meat to make the neat cutlet. Gradually, leftover sabzis (curries) found their way into becoming a cutlet.

The heritage hub Indian Coffee House in Kolkata popularised cutlets, the finger food eaten with chai when intellectuals met up for an adda session, rather like a 'hang-out' or a casual conversation between like-minded people. Whatever their origins and history, fried cutlets in all forms are eaten all over India. The vegetarian ones are made with cooked vegetables, including potatoes, peas, beans and carrots, mixed with spices, flattened into small round patties and shallow-fried. In this chapter, there's an aloo tikki recipe and a vegetable cutlet recipe.

As nostalgic as pakoras and cutlets is the Parle-G biscuit, easily identified by its yellow-striped packaging and plump Parle-G baby on the front. Every Indian has memories of dunking these biscuits in chai and eating them before they become all soggy – people even call Parle-G an emotion. In my opinion, these sweet, sugary biscuits don't pair with chai as well as savoury spicy snacks, but they were the first ever biscuit produced by India in 1939, when imported brands such as United Biscuits, Huntley & Palmers, Britannia and Glaxo dominated the market and were only consumed by the elite due to their price point. The launch of Parle-G (at the time called Parle-Gluco – now the 'G' stands for glucose) was 'not just a business decision but also a responsibility to sell affordable biscuits to Indians (during British rule) at a time the market was flooded with costly imports', said Ajay Chauhan, executive director at Parle Products. Parle-G is the world's best-selling biscuit, according to the Nielsen Corporation, surpassing the likes of Oreo. It is estimated that over a billion packets are sold each month. Although I didn't grow up in India, I have memories of

eating these biscuits daily during the first Ram Katha (spiritual festival – see page 129) I attended in India at the age of twelve. There was a group of around twenty of us from abroad who would be eating these before the katha began in the morning, passing them around as we sat on the banks of the Narmada river in Sisodra, a small village in Gujarat, with over a hundred thousand people attending daily.

Breakfasts

Masala Omelette

There are ample variations of the masala omelette, also known as desi omelette, 'desi' meaning 'of our home country'. You'll find this spiced omelette prepared by street vendors in India, with coriander, onions, tomatoes, green chillies and any other spices they like. A savoury and spicy dish, this is perfect paired with a cup of sweet, milky chai.

Serves 1

1 tablespoon oil, ghee or butter
½ teaspoon cumin seeds
¼ onion or 2 tablespoons, sliced or chopped
½–1 green chilli, finely chopped
2 tablespoons coriander leaves, chopped
a pinch turmeric powder (optional)
¼ teaspoon salt
½ tomato or a few cherry tomatoes, chopped
2 large eggs, beaten

Heat the oil, ghee or butter in a medium frying pan, add the cumin seeds and let them go a little brown, then stir-fry the onion, chilli and coriander leaves for a couple of minutes. Then add in the turmeric powder, if using, salt and tomatoes and give it all a quick stir. Spread out the mixture in the pan so it's evenly spread and pour the beaten eggs over the top. Let this cook on a medium heat until it sets, and is beginning to colour on the bottom and is slightly crisp around the edges. Flip the omelette over and cook for a minute on the other side. Once set, fold it over and serve with toast, roti, paratha or anything you like.

Tofu Bhurji

You normally get bhurji made with eggs – it's a street-side breakfast favourite in India, served, of course, with a cup of sweet chai. Think scrambled eggs but with the addition of plenty of spices. Tofu takes on the flavour of spices in the same way as eggs do, so here's the vegan version of Egg bhurji. I like using silken tofu for this as its consistency seems egg-like, but if using firm tofu, simply crumble it into the tempered spices in the same way, as explained below.

Serves 4

1 block/350g silken tofu
1 teaspoon oil
½ teaspoon mustard seeds
1 medium red onion, finely chopped
1 clove garlic, grated or chopped (optional)
½ green chilli, finely chopped (optional)
¼ teaspoon turmeric powder
salt to taste
a handful (around 10) almonds, roughly chopped
a handful coriander, finely chopped

To serve:
brown toast or buns

Start by leaving the tofu on a few kitchen towels or tissues to let the excess water drain for as long as possible, anything from 10 minutes to 2 hours.

When you're ready to cook the scramble, melt the oil in a flat-based pan on low heat, then add the mustard seeds and wait until they sizzle before adding the onions.

Stir and let the onions go brown, then add the garlic, green chilli and turmeric powder, and stir for another 15 seconds.

Now break the tofu into the pan and mix together, add the salt, almond pieces and coriander. You can let this cook for anything from 5 to 15 minutes, then serve on toast.

Chickpea-flour Corn Fritters

Here's a filling savoury breakfast or brunch option, served up with yoghurt chutney. You can also add smashed avocado or a fried or poached egg on top. The possibilities are endless. Chickpea flour makes this dish lighter, plus it's naturally gluten-free and higher in protein than other flours.

Makes 10–12 mini fritters

For the batter:
½ cup/80g sweetcorn kernels
½ cup/50g chickpea flour/gram flour
50ml water
1 spring onion, sliced or 2 tablespoons chopped onions
½ teaspoon black pepper
¾ teaspoon salt
2 tablespoons lemon or lime juice
½ teaspoon curry powder
½ teaspoon paprika
⅛ teaspoon baking powder
a handful coriander leaves (optional)
1 green chilli, finely chopped (optional)

For the yoghurt chutney:
2 tablespoons yoghurt
pinch of salt
¼ teaspoon or less of chilli powder

Mix all the ingredients for the batter together, taste for salt, chilli, lime and make any adjustments. Heat a flat pancake pan, pour in some oil (around 1 teaspoon) and let this heat up on a low to medium heat. Now take a tablespoon of the batter and place it on the pan to make each fritter. Spread them out on the oil and let them cook until brown on one side, then flip them over and let them cook on the other side. Mix together the chutney ingredients and serve.

Bateta Poha

This is a comforting brunch dish I've grown up eating, especially on weekends – it's savoury, lightly tangy and can be a little spicy, and is made of poha (flattened rice) with small pieces of potato. This is the way my mum makes it, which I absolutely love – in my opinion, the best poha I've ever had.

Serves 2

1 cup/150g poha
5 tablespoons oil
1 teaspoon cumin seeds
½ teaspoon mustard seeds
a handful curry leaves
1 medium onion, finely chopped
1 green chilli, slit lengthways
1 medium/200g potato, peeled and chopped
    into small cubes
pinch of turmeric
¼ teaspoon garam masala
salt to taste
juice of ½ a lemon or lime

First, wash the poha thoroughly in cold running water to remove any excess starch then set aside. Now heat the oil in a pan, add the cumin seeds and mustard seeds and let them pop, then add curry leaves, onions and slit green chilli, stir for a few seconds, and lastly add the potato pieces. Stir well and let them cook on a low to medium heat, placing the lid on the pan until the potato pieces are cooked (around 8–10 minutes). Now stir in the washed poha. Add the turmeric, garam masala, salt and lemon or lime juice and stir lightly to ensure it doesn't become mushy.

Cheese and Onion Fritters with Green Chilli

These taste like a pancake version of chilli cheese toast, and are made with chickpea flour, so are healthier, easier to digest and, of course, naturally gluten-free. You can make these as spicy as you like by adding more green chillies, or you can eat them with your favourite sauce or chutney. They taste great by themselves too – fresh and hot, of course!

Makes 6–8 fritters

For the fritters:
⅔ cup/80g chickpea flour
pinch bicarbonate of soda
½ cup/110–120ml water
1 teaspoon vinegar
¼ teaspoon salt
oil for cooking
ground black pepper

Toppings:
½ onion, finely chopped
3–5 tablespoons Cheddar cheese, grated
1 green chilli, finely sliced
a handful coriander leaves, chopped

Mix the chickpea flour and bicarbonate of soda, then add the water little by little, mixing quickly with a spoon, fork or your fingers as you add. Add the vinegar and salt and whisk or mix well until the batter is smooth and of a thick, runny consistency.

Heat a flat pancake pan, pour in some oil (around ½ teaspoon) and let this heat up on a low to medium heat. Now take 2 tablespoons of the batter and place on the pan to make each fritter, like a mini pancake. Make sure each one has a little oil so it cooks well. Additionally, pour a few drops of oil around each fritter. Now add the toppings: sprinkle 1–2 teaspoons of chopped onions, a handful of grated cheese, a few green chilli slices and coriander leaves on each one. Sprinkle a little black pepper on each one. After a few minutes, once the underside is light brown and cooked, flip and cook on the other side. Serve hot with chai. You can serve with a sauce or chutney if you like, such as a coriander chutney or tomato ketchup.

Chai story: Teenage dhaba diaries

GUJARAT, 2000

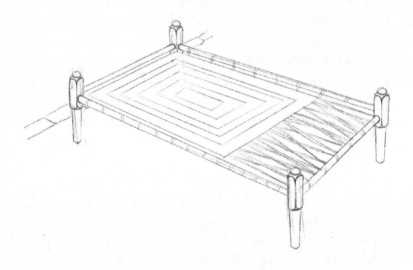

During a month-long trip in Gujarat in the summer between my A-level years, my brother Prashant – only a year younger than me – and I hired a car and driver and set off to explore different parts of the state we come from. We had no set agenda and no bookings – this was my dad's idea (and directive), as most of my memorable journeys in India were. Being an Indian street food and spice lover, my brother stopped at a busy roadside stall one evening, just as we were leaving the city of Rajkot on an overnight car journey, to have samosa dabeli. This is possibly the most flavourful must-have roadside snack in these parts: sweet, spicy and sour from the accompanying masalas and chutneys, delicious downed with a cup of super-sweet chai, which the chaiwala next door ceremoniously and adeptly poured from a large aluminium

pot, lifting it high as he poured the piping-hot chai into small chai glasses. He served it with a white rakabi, or saucer. We slurped our chai from the rakabis and made each other laugh.

'Dabeli', meaning 'pressed down' in Gujarati, is an Indian burger, with a tasty potato filling, chutneys, crunchy sev, masala peanuts and pomegranate pearls pressed inside a white bun, similar to a popular snack known as Vada pav, found on the streets of Mumbai. The contrast of chutneys and spices makes it sweet and sour, the sev adds a crunch to the otherwise soft bun and the dabeli masala has a unique flavour made from a blend of dried red chillies, black pepper, dried coconut, clove, cinnamon, coriander seeds, cumin seeds, star anise, turmeric, cardamom, bay leaves, black salt and more, a mix that is now easy to find in supermarkets and online. It is this special masala that really sets this dish or burger apart, just as the spice combinations used in different Indian dishes make each one taste so unique. The dabeli has its own masala, so does pau bhaji, and chickpea curry, which uses chana masala – these spice blends come ready in packs.

Dabeli was originally created in the town of Mandavi from the Kutchh region, but now you can find it all over Mumbai, Rajasthan, even in Delhi and other parts of India. While the potato dabeli is the original and most common, there's also a samosa-stuffed dabeli, where a whole crispy samosa filled with chopped vegetables is squashed between the two sides of the bun with the chutneys, crunchy sev, onions, dabeli masala and all the rest.

I have never been as adventurous as Prashant when it comes to food, or able to take as much spice; and so it was again that day. I must have been more affected by the chutneys (the only raw ingredient in the dish, made with local water, best avoided especially in the monsoon season), and a few hours after devouring the dabeli for dinner, as we yawned and slept through the bumpy car ride to another city, I felt sick and we had to stop.

It must have been two in the morning when we drew up next to a dhaba, a streetside restaurant usually found on highways and open all day and night, this time in the middle of nowhere. While my brother went to have a second dinner, I used the dim torch on my Nokia phone to walk into what seemed like an open field with very tall grass to squat, a better and cleaner option – though slightly more precarious both in terms of insects and people – than the dhaba bathroom. I knew the latter would be intolerable, especially as I was already feeling sick. We asked the driver to keep watch and make sure no one came, but I still had a gulp of fear as I squatted in the dark, and then, as soon as I was done, ran back and crossed the road to the dhaba, where my brother's dal had just been served. Our driver drank plenty of chai – the tea at dhabas has to be strong, a sure way to keep sleep at bay on long overnight journeys.

I kicked off my flat sandals, sat cross-legged on the charpoy and sighed. Some dhabas still have these old 'charpoys', rustic traditional beds with four short legs held together with coir ropes that bind the frame tightly, although many have sadly replaced them with cheap plastic chairs and tables. Dhabas came about on either side of the Grand Trunk Road, one of Asia's oldest and longest roads, linking the eastern and western regions of the Indian subcontinent, also the busiest route for trade between Amritsar and Lahore, during the twentieth century, mainly to serve truckers. The menus originally reflected the fact that most came from Punjab, but with dhabas all over India now, this has, of course, changed. Dhabas are now an essential pitstop for all travellers and an important part of the food scene, with people even travelling specifically to certain famous dhabas for particular dishes.

I couldn't eat anything, of course, but watched as my brother tore into the freshly cooked buttered roti and slurped the hot *yellow daal, studded with plenty of green chillies. At that time, I couldn't eat half as much spice as him, so he was happy to be ordering a much spicier daal all for himself, not having to share it. Thankfully we both slept well on the four-hour onward journey to Porbandar.*

Sandwiches and Toasts

Avo-on-Toast with Roasted Red Pepper Spread

Roasting red peppers transforms them, makes them deliciously soft and sweet and brings out the flavour. So blending the roasted peppers into a chutney gives it real depth of flavour and warmth. The addition of walnuts makes it creamy, nutty and rather like the Middle-Eastern muhammara dip. This is a hearty sauce, delicious on any bread and a beautiful pop of colour with the avocado.

Serves 2

For the red pepper spread (makes 1 small jar):
2 red peppers
1 tomato or 5 cherry tomatoes
a handful (around 5) walnuts
1 tablespoon oil
¼ teaspoon salt
½ teaspoon cumin seeds (optional)
¾ teaspoon chilli flakes
½ teaspoon paprika
1 clove garlic (optional)

For the toast:
2 slices of sourdough, wholegrain or any bread you like, toasted
1 avocado, sliced or chopped
sesame seeds or furikake (Japanese seasoning) mix

Preheat the oven to 180°C/350°F/gas mark 4. Cut up the red peppers, discard the seeds and roughly chop the tomato. Mix the red peppers, tomatoes and walnuts in the oil, salt and cumin seeds, then roast them in the oven for 30 minutes. Once cooked, place the red peppers, tomatoes and the rest of the ingredients in a blender and blend until a smooth paste is formed. Taste and add salt or chilli if needed. Spread on toast, add a few slices of avocado and top with some sesame seeds, furikake or any seed mix you like.

Tip: Use smoked paprika if you want more of a smoky, barbecued flavour.

Bombay Sandwich with Sweet Potato

Covering all flavours of sweet, savoury and spicy, this toasted sandwich is traditionally made with cooked potato slices, although I've used mashed sweet potato here, as well as onions, tomatoes, chillies, and layers of coriander chutney, cheese and tomato ketchup. Chaat masala is the essential ingredient here – a dry spice blend you can get ready-made which is used in a variety of snacks and dishes. It is zingy and tangy, and a mix of various spices, but the most distinctive flavour is the sulphurous black salt, as well as the fruity and citrusy amchur powder, made from dried unripe mangoes.

You will need a toasted-sandwich maker for this.

Serves 2

4 small or medium slices of bread

For the sweet potato:
1 medium sweet potato, boiled or steamed and mashed
¾ teaspoon chaat masala
1 teaspoon olive oil
salt to taste
1 teaspoon roasted cumin seeds (optional)

Other ingredients:
a few slices each of tomato, cucumber, onions
½ avocado, sliced (optional)
2 tablespoons grated cheese
butter, to spread

For the coriander chutney:
a large handful coriander leaves
1–2 tablespoons peanuts (or soaked cashews), chopped
1 tablespoon yoghurt (optional)
¼ teaspoon salt
a squeeze of lemon or lime
1 green chilli, if you like it spicy, finely chopped
1–2 teaspoons sugar

Mix together the ingredients for the coriander chutney; you can do this in advance. Combine together all the ingredients for the sweet potato and mix well. To make the sandwiches, spread the coriander chutney on one side of the bread, make a thin layer of the sweet potato mash, layer the tomato, cucumber, onion and avocado slices. Sprinkle some grated cheese on top. Place another slice of bread on top, then toast in a sandwich toaster. If you don't have a sandwich toaster, simply toast both slices of bread before layering the ingredients inside.

Chilli Cheese Toast

A deliciously indulgent and heart-filling accompaniment to chai, this toast is topped with a mix of cheese, butter, green chillies and onions, then grilled and topped again with chilli flakes. There are, of course, variations in toppings. You can add sweetcorn, red pepper, tomatoes and garlic if you like. This snack comes from Mumbai and was apparently invented by Satish Arora when he was the executive chef of the Taj Mahal Hotel. An article in the *Hindustan Times* quotes him on how he created it around 1975–6. 'It was just by accident,' he said. 'I was having tea with my sous chefs when I tried grated Amul cheese with chopped onions, chopped hard tomatoes, chopped coriander leaves. I mixed it well. I put it on an ordinary slice of white bread and put it in the salamander (grill).' The dish now turns up on every menu, from fancy hotels to roadside stalls. London's Dishoom restaurant is now famous for its chilli cheese toast for breakfast, so much so that it is now on the all-day menu.

Serves 1

1 slice of bread
1 heaped teaspoon butter
1 small green chilli, finely chopped
a handful chopped coriander
1 spring onion or ½ small onion, chopped
a sprinkle of salt and black pepper
a handful/5 tablespoons grated cheese

Lightly grill or toast the bread on both sides. Mix together the butter, chilli, coriander, onions, salt and pepper in a small mixing bowl. Spread this mixture on the grilled bread and add grated cheese on top so the bread is full covered. Sprinkle some more chopped onions on top of the cheese. Sprinkle some chilli flakes to add colour and place under the grill for 3–5 minutes until golden brown.

Masala Beans on Toast

When my family, along with so many others, came to this country as immigrants and as vegetarians, they mainly lived on bread, chips, beans and mushy peas. There wasn't much Indian food available, so they made their own spiced-up versions of dishes. Baked beans are already cooked, hence easy to adapt, and they have that savoury-sweet combination that Indians love, so, by adding spices, a touch of chilli and cooking them with onions, they became a cheap, simple and tasty Indian-flavoured treat, a bit like curried baked beans. My grandmother used to make these masala baked beans as a curry with roti many years ago, while other Indian families I know made it as a breakfast dish served with toast or with an omelette. Once you try this, I'm sure you'll want to make it again!

Serves 2

1–2 teaspoons oil
1 teaspoon cumin seeds
¼ onion, roughly chopped
1 garlic clove, grated
1 green chilli, finely chopped
1 tablespoon tomato purée
½ teaspoon garam masala
¼ teaspoon turmeric powder
1 tin baked beans (415g)
salt to taste
a handful coriander leaves

For the toast:
2 slices of sourdough, wholegrain or any bread you like,
    toasted

Optional toppings:
1 spring onion, chopped, or a small handful of finely
    chopped onion
1 green chilli, finely chopped or sliced
a handful grated cheese

Heat the oil in a pan, add the cumin seeds and let them sizzle
on a low to medium heat for 15 seconds or so before adding the
chopped onions. Stir well and let the onions become slightly
brown, then stir in the grated garlic and green chilli pieces.
Now add the tomato purée, garam masala and turmeric powder,
stir for 5–10 seconds and then stir in the baked beans and salt.
Cook for a few minutes on a low heat – if you cook for too
long, the beans will dry out, in which case just add a little water
to make it a juicy consistency. Stir in the chopped coriander
leaves, leaving some for garnishing.

Toast your bread, layer with the masala baked beans, add any
optional toppings and enjoy.

Tip: If you're topping your toast with cheese, you can also grill
the toast with all the toppings or simply let it melt on the hot
beans.

Sweet Figs and Spiced Yoghurt on Toast

I love biting into sweetness and spice, and this combination of fresh figs, sweet balsamic and spicy yoghurt topped with chopped red chillies is a perfect blend of contrasting flavours. This tadka yoghurt is something I've been making for years in different variations, and it works well as a dressing, a spread or a chutney. If you prefer it mild, then simply omit the chillies when making the tadka.

Serves 2

5 fresh figs
2 sourdough or any bread slices, toasted
a drizzle of balsamic reduction
a few red chillies, chopped (optional)
coriander leaves

For the tadka yoghurt:
1 teaspoon oil
¼ teaspoon mustard seeds
¼ teaspoon cumin seeds
½ green chilli, finely chopped
1 teaspoon sesame seeds
¼ teaspoon salt
5 tablespoons/150g thick yoghurt

You can prepare the yoghurt sauce in advance and keep it ready in the fridge. To make this, place the oil in a small pan with the mustard and cumin seeds and cook on a low heat. Once the mustard seeds and cumin seeds start popping, add the chopped green chilli and sesame seeds and remove from the heat quickly (let the sesame seeds become slightly brown). Pour this mix into the yoghurt, add the salt and mix well.

Slice the figs when you are preparing the toast so they remain fresh. Spread the yoghurt on the toasted bread and top with a few fig slices. Now add a drizzle of balsamic reduction and a few chopped red chillies, if using, as well as coriander leaves.

Tip: You can use balsamic vinegar, but the reduction is more syrupy and sweeter, so gives the toast a lovely sweetness.

Chai story: Hot peanuts

KURUKSHETRA, 2022

It's a cool November evening in Kurukshetra, and after another day of katha, my friend Mukund and I are driving to see our guru, Morari Bapu. We spot a man stirring singh dana (peanut shells) in a large deep pan, wafts of smoke escaping into the air, and beside him, a cart filled with mounds of peanuts, ready to buy. The pan is tilted towards the road to lure passers-by with the fragrant, warming, nutty aroma, so we stop the car to get some for Bapu, 500g for 70 rupees, around 70 pence. The vendor swiftly wraps the nuts in two sheets of a newspaper and hands the package over.

Kurukshetra is in the northern state of Haryana, a place of spiritual and religious significance, as this is where Krishna spoke the words of the Bhagavad Gita *to Arjuna, on this battlefield.*

Many make a pilgrimage to connect with this historical land, to take a dip in the holy water of Brahma Sarovar, to tie a string on the branches of a beautiful banyan tree, under which it is said that Krishna spoke the Gita, and to see the battlefield where the war between the two groups of cousins, the Kauravas and the Pandavas, in one of the most important Hindu epics, the Mahabharata, *took place.*

I'm in this city for Morari Bapu's Ram Katha, which I have been listening to ever since I was a child. Bapu speaks on the Ramayana (the Ram Charit Manas) *all over India and the world. This particular katha is taking place on the Kurukshetra battlefield. He speaks for three to four hours in the morning, and on some evenings, like today, he meets people, or rather has a small gathering where he might speak, or there might be a performance, either music or dance or poetry. Tonight is more intimate, with a smaller group of people, where Bapu is simply sitting and remembering his younger years as a kathakar travelling the world.*

As we approach his living room – his house, or what is called a kutiya, is a small, slightly elevated structure in the garden – the remnants of smoke from Bapu's havan fire ritual float towards us, a familiar burning smell that will forever remind me of him. I smile. The embers inside the square-shaped havan flicker away as we enter. Bapu nods and smiles, ushering us in, the left lens of his glasses reflecting the golden light of the cinders. Bapu sits on a white hindoro swing in one corner, in front of a brown thatched wall, a few of his close followers, who he doesn't like calling followers but instead calls 'flowers', sitting in front of him. I find a place in front of one of the small heaters, which radiate more orange light in the room.

Small paper cups of chai are being handed out and passed around while Bapu sips on his own garam chai, always served to him in a wooden bowl called a patra. The larger surface area of

the bowl allows the chai to cool quickly, as Bapu likes to drink it
piping hot. He is sitting with his light brown sandhya, or evening
shawl, wrapped around him fully, one arm inside, as the evenings
are getting colder now. Chai here in the north of India, I've realised recently, is milkier and less kadak, or strong – it seems that
the strength of chai is weaker in the northern states, they also use
only grated ginger and whole cardamom pods, sometimes also
adding saunf, or fennel seeds, without additional powdered spice
blends, thus it is slightly less spicy, as the powdered spice blends
give a much stronger and spicier flavour. Such different chai to
what we are used to as Gujaratis, where kadak chai with an
abundance of spices is more the order of the day. As Gujaratis,
we also grew up drinking kadak chai, not knowing that anything
less strong would even pass as Indian tea. But it seems that chai
everywhere is very different.

My friend hands forward the singh dana we bought earlier,
which is passed from hand to hand, until it reaches Bapu. There's
over fifty of us in the room, a very small audience compared to the
hundreds of thousands at the morning katha each day. He opens
the bag and takes a few, the crack of the shell piercing the silence,
and then passes it to the man sitting in front of him to pass it
around to the followers. I listen to Bapu over the sounds of nuts
being snapped and opened, as he speaks about his younger days,
before he became as well known as he is today, how he travelled,
what he carried in his small hand luggage with no check-in bag-
gage, and his encounters with other religious leaders.

Bapu suddenly remembers the food left over from bhiksha
today, which he has just come from, and asks for the organisers
to pass it around. Bhiksha is a ritual still followed by saints in
which they find a small house on the road and ask the family to
make chai and a meal using 'gangajal', or water of the Ganges,
which Bapu always carries with him – he only drinks this water

and only eats food made with it. Sometimes, the family recognises Bapu, but many times they don't, yet they oblige, considering it a privilege to feed a saint, at the end of which Bapu gives them prashad, a gift, in the form of money.

The steel container has at least five thick rotis – again, the rotis in the north of India are much heavier and thicker than how we as Gujaratis eat them, perhaps because of the colder climate here – there is a doodhi, or bottle gourd curry, lying on top, and a large block of gor, gud (pronounced differently by everyone) or jaggery, hard yet soft around the edges. I snap a large chunk of the jaggery and a section of a roti and eat them together, one of my favourite combinations from when I was a child. As I bite into the earthy, rich sweetness of the gor, I wish I'd taken more.

Snacks

Peanut Chaat

This makes for a bright and colourful appetiser with all the contrasting colours, flavours and textures. To create it, peanuts are tossed with vegetables, fruit, fragrant spices and tangy lemon and coriander. If you want to make this but haven't had the time to soak the peanuts, just use ready-roasted salted peanuts and mix together all the ingredients, omitting the extra salt.

Makes 1 large bowl, around 6–8 portions

1 cup/100g peanuts
water
½ teaspoon salt

For the tempering (optional step):
1 teaspoon oil
1 teaspoon cumin seeds
5–6 curry leaves

For the chaat:
½ onion, finely chopped
5 cherry tomatoes or 1 small tomato, chopped
chunk of cucumber, around ⅛ large cucumber,
    finely chopped
2 tablespoons sweetcorn (optional)
1 tablespoon coriander leaves, chopped
½ green chilli, finely chopped
1 teaspoon chaat masala
2 teaspoons lemon or lime juice

Soak the peanuts overnight in water, ensuring that the water comes up to about 2–3 inches above the levels of the peanuts, and boil the next day for 20 minutes with the salt on a low to medium heat. Strain the water and let them cool down. If you haven't managed to soak the peanuts, cook them for longer in the water, around 1–2 hours, until soft.

Tempering the peanuts is optional, but it certainly adds to the flavour. Simply heat the oil in a pan, add the cumin seeds, let them become brown and then add the curry leaves. Stir for 10 seconds or so before adding the peanuts. Toss together for a minute and then leave aside.

Mix together the peanuts and the rest of the chaat ingredients, taste and make any adjustments.

Corn Chaat

A chaat is a medley of lip-smacking flavours and contrasting textures and vibrant colours, hence the word 'chaat', which literally translates as 'to lick' or 'to taste'. Corn chaat is possibly simpler than other chaats and, as always, there are different ways to make it. This is a tangy mixture of sweetcorn with onions, tomatoes, the very important chaat masala, herbs, spices and sev – a thin noodle-type crispy snack made from gram flour found all over India and in many Indian stores and large supermarkets in the UK.

Makes 1 large bowl, around 6–8 portions

1 tin/340g corn (285g drained weight)
    or 2 corn on the cobs
1 teaspoon butter
1 teaspoon cumin seeds
½ onion, finely chopped
½ pepper, finely chopped
1 tomato, finely chopped
juice of ½ a lemon or lime
salt to taste
½ teaspoon black pepper
½ teaspoon chaat masala
a handful coriander, finely chopped
1 green chilli, finely chopped
a handful sev

If using corn on the cob, cook the cob on a naked flame or under the grill, moving regularly so that it becomes brown on all sides. Now shuck the cob, slicing the kernels from each side. Melt the butter in a pan with the cumin seeds for a minute before adding the shucked corn. Cooking in a pan is also an optional step. You can mix everything together cold and serve as a cold chaat too. Now transfer into a mixing bowl and add all the ingredients apart from the sev. Mix well, taste and make any adjustments. Garnish with sev and some more coriander leaves. Make sure you put the garnish on when about to serve or eat as the sev needs to be crispy.

Aloo Tikki – Potato and Pea Cutlet

A popular street food throughout India, aloo tikki is a smashed potato and pea cutlet that can also be made with potatoes only, pan-fried with a few spices in a little oil. Delicious comfort food! You can eat alone with chai or dip them in a little ketchup, or green coriander chutney.

Makes 20–22 tikkis

6 small potatoes or 2 large potatoes (around 400g),
    unpeeled
¼ teaspoon salt
⅔ cup/100g peas
a few tablespoons of oil to cook the tikkis

For the tempering:
1 tablespoon oil
1 teaspoon cumin seeds
5–8 curry leaves
2 teaspoons sesame seeds
1 green chilli, finely chopped
1 inch piece ginger, grated
salt to taste
juice of ½ a small lemon or lime, or 1 tablespoon juice

If using large potatoes, chop into quarters so they're quicker to cook. Boil the potatoes, then cook in a pressure cooker or steam. If cooking in a pressure cooker, fill the water slightly above the level of the potatoes so that all the potatoes are fully covered. Add a little salt to the water. Pressure cook for 5–6 whistles on medium to medium-high heat (approximately 20 minutes).

In another small pan, boil the peas for 5 minutes, then drain the water and let them cool down until the potatoes are cooked. Now make the tempering. Heat the oil in a small pan, add the cumin, curry leaves, sesame seeds, green chilli and ginger. Let them crackle for a few seconds before removing from the heat and adding the salt and lemon or lime.

Once cooled a little, peel the potatoes (the skin should come off easily), place them in a mixing bowl with the peas and the spice tempering, and mash.

Now roll the mixture into small balls the size of a golf ball, and flatten them. The tikkis should be around 2 inches/5cm diameter.

Add 2 tablespoons oil to a pan and cook around 10 tikkis at a time. Let the oil heat to a low heat, then place the tikkis on the pan one by one, letting them cook on one side until they become crispy and brown (around 5–8 minutes), then turn and let them cook until brown on the other side. Serve hot or let cool and serve later with ketchup and chilli sauce.

Vegetable Cutlets

You'll find this traditional, deliciously crispy yet soft savoury accompaniment to chai at Indian roadside stalls, made with different vegetables like potatoes, green beans, carrots, sweetcorn and cabbage, mixed with spices and shallow-fried in oil.

Makes 10–15 cutlets, depending on size

2 tablespoons oil
1 teaspoon cumin seeds
1 medium potato (around 200g) chopped into
    very small cubes
½ cup/80g frozen peas
1 carrot, chopped into small pieces
1 teaspoon sugar
salt to taste
juice of ½ a lemon or lime
3 tablespoons chopped coriander leaves
1 green chilli, finely chopped (optional)
¼ teaspoon garam masala
1 medium onion, finely chopped
1 tablespoon plain flour
small bowl breadcrumbs
oil for cooking the cutlets, around 1 tablespoon

Serve with:
tomato ketchup and chilli sauce

Start by heating the oil in a large pan, then add the cumin seeds. Once they are cooked and sizzling, add the potatoes, peas and carrots and let them cook on a low heat for around 15 minutes until soft. Keep the lid on the pan and stir regularly.

Now add the sugar, salt, lemon or lime juice, coriander leaves, chilli (if using), garam masala and onion. Stir well, remove from the heat and mash the vegetables. Taste for salt, lime and sugar and make any adjustments. Add the plain flour and mix well so it almost becomes a dough.

Now divide into rounds or triangular cutlets (2 inches long) and cover in breadcrumbs. Heat a flat pan and add 1 tablespoon oil. Once hot, move the oil so it covers the pan and place the cutlets on the oil. Let them go brown on one side, then flip over to the other side. Serve hot with ketchup or chilli sauce, or any sauce you like, and always with a cup of chai.

Hondvo Mini Muffins

Hondvo, also known as handvo, is a quintessentially Gujarati baked dish, made with various flours, grated vegetables and spices, topped with crisp sesame seeds. Here's a much easier and simpler version of it, made with courgettes and carrots, a batter you can simply mix up and put in the oven (traditionally handvo is fermented overnight, so making it is quite a process). It goes so perfectly with chai and lasts for days! These also make for great picnic additions, they're good to have in your bag on a day out, and can be kept in the fridge for 4–5 days.

Makes 8–10 mini muffins

1 cup/100g plain flour
⅓ cup/50g olive oil
¼ teaspoon baking powder
¼ teaspoon bicarbonate of soda
½ cup of almond or any plant milk you like
¼ teaspoon turmeric
1 spring onion, sliced or 1 tablespoon white onion,
    finely chopped
1 garlic clove, grated
small piece ginger, grated
½ green chilli, finely chopped (optional)
2 teaspoons sugar
salt to taste
juice of 1 lemon or lime
½ carrot, grated
½ small courgette, grated

For the tempering:
1 tablespoon oil
½ teaspoon mustard seeds
5–8 curry leaves
a pinch of asafoetida (optional)
1 tablespoon sesame seeds

To garnish:
a sprinkle of sesame seeds

Preheat the oven to 190°C/350°F/gas mark 5. Lightly brush the muffin pans with some oil or butter to prevent the batter from sticking to the tin once baked.

Mix together the ingredients for the batter. If you don't have plant milk, use water, as dairy milk cannot be mixed with lemon. If tempering the spices, heat the oil in a small pan on a low to medium heat, add the mustard seeds to the oil, once they start to pop, add the curry leaves, asafoetida and sesame seeds. Once the sesame seeds are a slightly darker brown (this should take less than a minute), pour this tempering into the cake batter and stir well. Taste the batter for salt, spice and sweetness. Pour the batter into your muffin tin, filling each case until half full, top with sesame seeds and place in the oven. Bake for 20–23 minutes. You can check that they are baked by piercing the muffins with a fork and, if it comes out clean, it's baked. Let them cool and then serve with a cup of chai.

Palak Pakora or Bhajia

The Indian pakora is an emotion, the epitome of comfort food, wrapped in crisp layers of besan or chickpea flour, perfectly paired with chai. It is what Indians crave on a rainy day. A fritter, rather like Japanese tempura, made with anything from vegetables to banana and fish. It has many forms and many names across the country, from bhajia as we Gujaratis call them to pakoras, pakori, bhajis and more. Pakoras are deep-fried, which is what makes them crispy, but I've shallow-fried these palak or spinach pakora in a pan, making them easier to make and, of course, lighter to eat. They're light, slightly crispy and savoury, and perfectly complemented by a cup of sweet chai.

Makes 12–15 pakoras

12–15 leaves of spinach

For the batter:
½ cup/50g chickpea/gram flour
¼ teaspoon salt
¼ teaspoon chilli powder (optional)
a pinch/⅛ teaspoon baking powder
¼ cup/50ml water
oil to cook

Mix together all the ingredients for the batter. Heat a flat pan, place 1 tablespoon oil in the pan and let the oil heat up on a low to medium heat. Now dip each spinach leaf in the batter so that it is fully coated on both sides and place in the hot oil. Make 5–6 leaves at a time to ensure there is enough oil for all the leaves. Once brown on one side, turn to cook on the other side. Transfer onto a plate, add more oil to the pan and cook the rest of the leaves. Serve with a cup of sweet and hot chai.

Pudla or Chilla

Known as 'pudla' in Gujarat and 'chilla' in Mumbai, these savoury chickpea-flour pancakes are served with coriander chutney and yoghurt. Indians, especially Gujaratis, use chickpea flour, also known as gram flour, for a whole range of tasty vegetarian snacks and meals. Chickpea flour is high in fibre and plant-based protein, keeping your blood-sugar levels balanced and helping you feel fuller for longer than a wheat-based white flour. Rather than using the ginger, garlic and chilli paste, you can grate 1 garlic clove, a small piece of ginger and some chopped chillies if you like it spicy.

Makes around 6 pudla and serves 2

For the pancakes:
1 cup/100g chickpea flour
1 tablespoon natural yoghurt
1 teaspoon ginger, garlic and chilli paste
a pinch of turmeric powder
½ teaspoon salt
½ cup/100ml water

Using your hand, thoroughly mix all the pudla pancake batter ingredients together in a mixing bowl until a smooth consistency batter is reached. To cook the pudla, take a medium-sized flat pan and place over a medium heat. Once the pan is warm, pour a large spoonful of the batter into the pan and spread evenly in circular clockwise motions using the back of the spoon, pressing very lightly so that no gap is created. Pour a few drops of oil on each side of the pudla so that it cooks properly. Once brown on the bottom side, use a wooden spatula to flip it and cook on the other side for a further minute. The pudla is cooked when a little browned on each side. Serve with coriander chutney (see page 241).

Pickles and Chutneys

Gor Keri

My mother would always bring back a large bottle of my nani's (maternal grandmother's) tangy and sweet gor keri from Loughborough whenever she went. This recipe is a diluted and much easier version of what my nani, who we called Baa, made (see page 95 for an explanation of how my nani made it, which is a longer process with fried spices and raw mango).

Achar masala, which is ready-made mix of pickle spices, is something you can source from any supermarket or online, although years ago, when Baa made gor keri, there was no achar masala. The sourness of the achar masala in this recipe is balanced by the naturally sweet jaggery, and it also adds a deep red colour to the pickle. You would only need a teaspoon to go with any savoury snack dish or even on toast.

Makes 1 jar

½ cup/100g jaggery
½ cup/125ml lemon juice
⅓ cup/100g pickle masala/achar masala

Mix together the above ingredients and leave for a few hours. Store in an airtight jar. This should last for a month or two in an airtight jar, depending on how often and how much you eat it.

Coriander Chutney

This is a staple chutney with any Indian dish, the perfect complement to sandwiches, cutlets, chaat, dhokla, pudlas and bhajias. You'll find this chutney at most Indian restaurants and most Indian homes. My mother makes a large batch of this and stores it in lots of small containers in the freezer, ready to be defrosted and used whenever needed.

Makes 1 jar

1 cup/25g coriander leaves
10–15 peanuts
1 teaspoon cumin seeds
1 clove garlic
½ teaspoon salt
juice of ½ lime
1–2 green chillies
1–2 teaspoons sugar
6 tablespoons water

Blend together all the ingredients until you have a thick, smooth liquid. Taste, make any adjustments and blend again if required. This will keep for 7–10 days in the fridge.

Red Chilli Chutney

This is a very simple and spicy chutney made with red chilli powder that takes no time to make and works well with everything. You can serve it alone with a dish or alongside the coriander chutney, for contrasting colours and flavours.

Makes 1 jar

2 tablespoons lemon or lime juice
1 tablespoon jaggery
¼ teaspoon sea salt
4 teaspoons red chilli powder

Mix together all the ingredients using a small whisk. The jaggery should mix in with a spoon, but if it is too coarse or hard then use the small side of a grater to grate it into the mix. This will help to dissolve it into the chutney. The chutney will keep for 7–10 days in the fridge in an airtight container.

Coconut Chutney

You'll find this served with most South Indian dishes, like dosa, idli and upma (see page 11). South India is full of coconut trees and so they use delicious fresh coconut, grated into the chutney. It's a much thicker chutney, with coconut pieces to bite on and lots of texture. You can serve it with anything you like!

Makes 1 large jar

1 cup/200g thick Greek yoghurt
2 tablespoons desiccated coconut, medium or large, according to taste
1 tablespoon coriander leaves, finely chopped
1 small green chilli, finely chopped
salt to taste

Mix together all the ingredients and water down a little if it's too thick. Taste for salt and chilli and make any adjustments.

Chai story: Breakfast at the Gurudwara

DELHI, 2022

It's a cold early morning in Delhi, still dark at 6 a.m. when my friend Gathika picks me up in her car. Interestingly, I visited her café last night, called Before the British Raj, as coffee was consumed in India before tea, hence before the British Raj. We drive to Bangla Sahib gurudwara, a place of worship for Sikhs. 'Look – the chai is right outside,' she tells me, as we drive past the chaiwala at the entrance. 'Chai after,' she smiles. There's steam rising into the cold air from the chai, beside which sits a full table of all kinds of fresh pakoras, from onions and chillies to spinach and bread fried in a chickpea-flour batter with spices, to have with chai.

I can't quite believe pakoras would be eaten for breakfast, but it is India, after all, and this is the epitome of comfort food for winter. I catch a glimpse of the golden dome of the gurudwara behind, beautifully carved, shining in the early-morning grey sky.

The sound of chanting, like a soft murmur, floats to us as we walk up the stairs from the car park, barefoot now – it's best to leave shoes in the car. I'm wearing socks, but as soon as I approach the steps of the gurudwara, a man asks me to remove my socks and leave them on the side. We step into the small pool of luke-warm water at the entrance to clean our feet, wiping them on the towel mat, then step onto the cold marble floor as we enter the gurudwara. The top of our heads are covered with a dupatta (scarf) as is customary, a sign of respect in the Sikh tradition. Gathika gets kada prasad for us, where she offers a donation and the gurudawa attendants give us a melt-in-the-mouth halwa oozing with ghee in recyclable bowls made of dried leaves. Half of this prasad is then taken to be offered to the gods. This halwa is served as divine prasad to all who visit the gurudwara, made with atta (flour), cooked in ghee and sweetened, of course, with sugar. As we leave the gurudwara, we are offered prasad again, this time in our hands, and this prasad has to be taken by all visitors.

This magnificent gurudwara was built in 1783 during the reign of Mughal Emperor Shah Alam II, to commemorate the visit of Guru Har Krishan, the eighth Sikh guru, in 1664. We touch the floor of the first step at the entrance with our right hand and then our eyes or our heart, something I've always done when entering temples or places of worship. We walk around the sacred shrine, where the holy book Guru Granth Sahib resides, and then out to the sarovar, or lake, whose water is said to be healing from the times of smallpox and cholera in the seventeenth century. The chanting from inside the gurudwara wafts over us, elevating the energy with a sense of the divine. As we leave, a man pours a little water into our hands from a silver teapot, which we drink and put over our heads.

As well as kada prasad, people can get langar, or meals, served at particular times in a hall below the gurudwara, from dal-chawal (lentil and rice) to sabzi-roti (vegetable and chapatis) and kheer (rice pudding), but they serve all meals including breakfast and tea. 'Seva', or selfless service, is very important in the Sikh world. During the first wave of Covid, the Bagla Sahib gurudwara fed 75,000 daily. Preparations began at 2 a.m. and the cooks worked through the day, especially during the lockdown periods, where volunteers weren't allowed inside, and so the staff worked 16–18 hours a day. The gurudwaras in India, including Bangla Sahib, were helping people with oxygen, refilling their oxygen cylinders, and they kept beds inside, a free and open service for all.

The skies are still grey as we walk outside, ready for our cup of morning chai. Delhi winter is gradually starting to set in. The steam from the chai draws me towards it. The chai looks more milky, and the colour is a light brown rather than the deeply coloured kadak chai I'm used to drinking in Mumbai and Gujarat, where I frequently travel. Chai is much more milky in this part of India, fewer tea leaves are used in the brew, and fewer spices, usually ginger, and perhaps some cardamom and saunf (fennel seeds). Even after all these years of travelling in India, I still think of Indian tea as always having to be kadak, but there really is no correct formula. I take the red clay kulhad cup from the chaiwala and sip the piping-hot chai – sweet, gingery, which I love, and rather milky. Warming and delicious, but it feels incomplete without the brown colour or strength from the tea leaves. My friend hands me the plate of pakora and I bite into one. This is methi palak pakora, made with fenugreek and spinach leaves, probably my favourite – it was my grandfather's favourite too, I remember with a smile.

Maybe it's because I just flew in yesterday and still feel half asleep, or it's the Delhi cold, but the pakora tastes divine right now, perfect with the sweet chai, despite the fact that this isn't breakfast food for me. But when in India, when in the Delhi winter, when sipping on garam chai at the break of dawn and when pakoras are as fresh as this . . . it makes for a more whole-some morning, complete even, a moment to savour. I wonder, as I take another slurp of chai, what went with pakora before Indians started drinking chai, or did pakoras come after chai? And what, indeed, happened before chai, not so long ago?

Chai is a ritual that feels so much a part of Indian culture and life that it seems steeped in history, yet it's a relatively new thing, a cultural phenomenon that has become synonymous with India. I hope, as I take another sip of chai and form yet another chai-inspired memory, that the meditative ritual of making chai, the tradition of drinking chai, the sound of slurping, the theatre of proud chaiwalas on the streets of India, the act of offering chai to guests, of both politics and heartbreak being discussed over chai, and all the variations of spice blends added to chai, will be passed down from generation to generation and live on – it is a drink that contains and arouses an entire spectrum of emotions, starting with a sigh.

References

Introduction

the earth's surface covered by tea plantations van Driem, George (2019) *The Tale of Tea: A Comprehensive History of Tea from Prehistoric Times to the Present Day* (Amsterdam: Brill Publishers)

the most popular beverage in the world, after water Stone, Daniel 'The world's top drink', *National Geographic*, published 28 April 2014

approximately 1.2 billion kilograms Data from https://www.statista.com/statistics/870829/india-consumption-volume-of-tea/

A Brief History of Tea

the spiritual tradition in China that . . . became Zen Buddhism Barua A. (2008) 'Romancing the *Camellia assamica* (Assam and the Story of Tea)' *Assam Rev. Tea News*, 18–27

where tea ceremonies were held Subramaniam, Bala (1995) *Tea in India* (New Delhi: Dr K.S. Krishnan Marg; Wiley Eastern)

the preferred currency in many parts of Central Asia MacFarlane, Alan and MacFarlane, Iris (2004) *Green Gold: The Empire of Tea* (London: Ebury)

the public sale of tea at the Sultaness Head in 1657 van Driem, George (2019) *The Tale of Tea: A Comprehensive History of Tea* *from Prehistoric Times to the Present Day* (Amsterdam: Brill Publishers)

material, medical, commercial, and culinary cultures Rappaport, Erika Diane (2017) *A Thirst for Empire* (Princeton: Princeton University Press)

the biggest drug cartel in the world Barua A. (2008) 'Romancing the *Camellia assamica* (Assam and the Story of Tea)' *Assam Rev. Tea News*, 18–27

the Treaty of Tientsin, which gave Britain Kowloon https://www.nationalarchives.gov.uk/education/resources/hong-kong-and-the-opium-wars/

the upper Brahmaputra Valley '200 years and counting, Assam's tea industry continues glory run', *Economic Times* https://economictimes.indiatimes.com/news/economy/agriculture/200-years-and-counting-assams-tea-industry-continues-glory-run/articleshow/97002225.cms

a first experiment Antrobus, H.A. (1957) *A History of Assam Company, 1839–1953* (Edinburgh: T. and A. Constable Ltd)

improved varieties of the native Assam plant Crole, David (1897) *A Textbook of Tea Planting and Manufacture* (London: Crosby Lockwood & Son)

on two sides of the world at the same time Rappaport, Erika Diane (2017) *A Thirst for Empire* (Princeton: Princeton University Press)

home to more than 6 million people Singh, Bikash 'Assam, India largest tea producer, working on a tea policy' *Economic Times*, published 19 October 2022, https://economictimes.indiatimes.com/news/economy/agriculture/assam-india-largest-tea-producer-working-on-a-tea-policy/articleshow/94970787.cms?utm_source=contentofinterest&utm_medium=text&utm_campaign=cppst

overwhelmed by disease and unfamiliar food Sharma, Jayeeta (2009) '"Lazy" Natives, Coolie Labour, and the Assam Tea

Industry' *Modern Asian Studies* 43:6, 1287–1324, https://sai. columbia.edu/sites/default/files/content/docs/Sharma,%20 Assam%20Tea%20Industry.pdf

turbulent, obstinate and rapacious Antrobus, H.A. (1957) *A History of Assam Company, 1839–1953* (Edinburgh: T. and A. Constable Ltd),

a profligate native . . . primitive virtues Sharma, Jayeeta (2009) '"Lazy" Natives, Coolie Labour, and the Assam Tea Industry', *Modern Asian Studies*, vol. 43, no. 6, pp. 1287–1324

notion of "primitivity" was crucial in categorising Bordoloi, Anisha (2015) 'Creating the "Primitive": A Study of British Colonialism and Migrant "Coolies" in the Tea Plantations of Assam Valley, 1860–1900', *International Journal of Social Science and Humanity*, 5:9 http://www.ijssh.net/papers/562-W00004. pdf

a generic category Varma, Nitin (2016) *Coolies of Capitalism: Assam Tea and the Making of Coolie Labour* (De Gruyter Oldenburg) https://doi.org/10.1515/9783110463170

as far as Madras and Bombay 'Annual Report on the Labour Immigration into Assam for the Year 1877', *Proceedings of the Dept of Revenue, Agriculture and Commerce*, December 1878

ancestors had never returned . . . social and economic change Sharma, Jayeeta (2009) '"Lazy" Natives, Coolie Labour, and the Assam Tea Industry' *Modern Asian Studies* 43:6, 1287–1324

respect for workers Sarin, Rekha and Kapoor, Rajan (2014) *Chai: The Experience of India Tea* (New Delhi: Niyogi Books)

the Indians influenced by them Doctor, Vikram 'Tea right choice' *Economic Times*, published 19 July 2006, https:// economictimes.indiatimes.com/tea-right-choice/articleshow/ 1773236.cms?from=mdr

religious, linguistic and caste groups Lutgendorf, Philip (2012) 'Making tea in India: Chai, capitalism, culture', *Thesis Eleven* 113 (1):11–31

A picker harvests almost 2,000–4,000 stems Sarin, Rekha and
Kapoor, Rajan (2014) *Chai: The Experience of Indian Tea* (New
Delhi: Niyogi Books)

Chai Ingredients

ginger has an enzyme that can curdle milk Trivedi-Grenier, Leena
'There's a Lot More to Masala Chai Than Spiced Milk Tea'
Epicurious, published 25 April 2021, https://www.epicurious.
com/expert-advice/masala-chai-history-recipe-article
resembling small acorns Van Wyk, Ben-Erik (2014) *Culinary
Herbs and Spices of the World* (London: Kew Publishing)
black tea may speed up our recovery Steptoe, A, Gibson,
E. Leigh, Vounonvirta, et al. (2007) 'The effects of tea on
psychophysiological stress responsivity and post-stress recovery:
a randomised double-blind trial', *Psychopharmacology*, 190:
81–89. See also: https://www.ucl.ac.uk/news/2006/oct/black-
tea-soothes-away-stress
the molecular fulcrum Bhattacharya, Tania 'The Indian
academic making the world look at flavours and food
in a fresh way' *National News*, published 25 April 2020,
https://www.thenationalnews.com/lifestyle/food/
the-indian-academic-making-the-world-look-at-flavours-and-
food-in-a-fresh-way-1.1010822
enhanced cognitive processing 'Spice up your holidays with brain-
healthy seasonings' Harvard Health blog, published 7 December
2016 https://www.health.harvard.edu/blog/spice-up-your-
holidays-with-brain-healthy-seasonings-2016120710734)
glycaemic control properties in diabetes Li, Y., Tran, V.H., Duke,
C. C. and Roufogalis, B.D. (2012) 'Preventive and Protective
Properties of *Zingiber officinale* (Ginger) in Diabetes Mellitus,
Diabetic Complications, and Associated Lipid and Other

Metabolic Disorders: A Brief Review', *Evid Based Complement.
Alternat. Med.* 2012: 516870, https://www.ncbi.nlm.nih.gov/
pmc/articles/PMC3519348/

cognitive processing in middle-aged women Saenghong, N. et
al. (2011) *'Zingiber officinale* Improves Cognitive Function of
the Middle-Aged Healthy Women', *Evid Based Complement.
Alternat. Med.* 2012: 383062, https://www.ncbi.nlm.nih.gov/
pmc/articles/PMC3253463/

delirium and tremors *Science Direct*, https://www.sciencedirect.
com/topics/pharmacology-toxicology-and-pharmaceutical-
science/nutmeg

on the Indian subcontinent Nair, Kodoth Prabhakaran (2020)
The Geography of Black Pepper The "King" of Spices, Volume 1
(Springer Nature Group)

to treat epileptic seizures Shaffer, Marjorie (2013) *Pepper –
A History of the World's Most Influential Spice* (New York:
Macmillan)

the severity of premenstrual syndrome Khazdair, M.R. et al.
(2015) 'The effects of *Crocus sativus* (saffron) and its
constituents on nervous system: A review' *Avicenna J Phytomed*
2015 Sep–Oct; 5(5): 376–391, https://www.ncbi.nlm.nih.gov/
pmc/articles/PMC4599112/

Chai accompaniments

executive director at Parle Products '73-year-old biscuit pioneer,
Parle-G becomes India's first homegrown Rs 5K crore FMCG
brand', *Economic Times*, published 13 February 2013 https://
economictimes.indiatimes.com/industry/cons-products/
fmcg/73-year-old-biscuit-pioneer-parle-g-becomes-indias-first-
homegrown-rs-5k-crore-fmcg-brand/articleshow/18473679.cms

Acknowledgements

Writing this book has required much research, reading and time, a very different process and indeed subject than my first two books. I've loved delving into history books and into my memories of India, and the research also led me to having some wonderful conversations and meetings with friends, friends of friends and people I've come across and connected with through books and online.

Thank you to everyone who spared the time to speak to me, sometimes more than once, and often when I had no real agenda, asking questions the conversation would guide me to ask, wondering what I might find out that could add some colour – or indeed spice – to my book.

My thanks to . . .

Anamika Singh, a second generation Tea Sommelier, Founder and Director of Anandini Himalaya Tea with over 30 years of working in the industry, for explaining the length and breadth of tea-growing through India, that 'life is held together in India by the two leaves and a bud.'

Akhil Sapru, vice chairman of J Thomas & Co Pvt Ltd, who helped me with the history and tea-making process. J Thomas & Co is the world's largest and oldest tea auctioneer, more than 170 years old, who organised the first tea auction outside of London, in Calcutta in 1861.

Deepti Dadlani, a good friend, founder of Mats & Chats, yoga therapist and educator, who took me to Mumbai's finest Taj Mahal Tea House years ago and talked me through all the regional Indian teas as I tasted them for a video I was creating.

Rishad Mehta, author of *Hot Tea Across India*, who, while I was writing this book, took me to his favourite Irani chai and brun maska spot in Mumbai, one of the few Irani cafes still left.

Arup K. Chatterjee (PhD), Professor of English, at Jindal Global University, who spent time discussing his concept of the gastromythology of English tea culture with me, and sent excerpts from his papers and his book.

The Library and Archives Team at the Royal Botanic Gardens, Kew, especially Anne Marshall, who kept a large stack of books on tea and spices ready for me to browse through every time I visited.

Gathika Chhabra, founder of Before British Raj, a wonderful café in Delhi I visited, which she has since expanded, who took me to a beautiful gurudwara at 6 a.m. the morning after she met me (see page 270 for the story)

Abhijit Bhattacharya from the Centre for Studies in Social Sciences, Calcutta, for sharing the iconic poster on page 37.

Priyanka Raj, my wonderful friend, for our chai discussions and for giving me three diverse books on tea from her collection. Priyanka organises brilliant events and pop-ups in Notting Hill, where she has lived for many years.

Stuart Cooper, my literary agent, who took me from a chai book idea (after exploring many other book ideas) to putting together a proposal and creating a structure, which I always find to be the most difficult part of writing a book.

Both my editors at Headline: Anna Steadman, who also edited my previous book *Prajñā* and decided to take on *The Book of Chai*; and Zoë Blanc, who edited much of this book, and guided me through the many drafts. I absolutely love the front cover, all thanks to Caroline Young, who also designed the front cover of *Prajñā*.

Thanks to this book, I learned and read about the British Empire, the history of India and of course how tea came about, because the latter is very much a part of the former. As children in English schools, we learned nothing about the Empire, and I hope this is changing now.

A huge thank you to my mother, Hema Manek, for helping me test the recipes and for making some of her delicious food for this book (and for all my books!) For all our delicious and healthy home recipes, see my first book *Saffron Soul*.

Lastly, I am grateful that, because of this book, I had a chance to delve into my grandmother's memories and ask her questions about growing up in a village in Gujarat, moving to Africa as a teenager and her travels to India as a mother of three young boys years later. I hope I've brought her stories to life for you and I hope this inspires you to ask your own grandparents about their childhood, their dreams and their lives – as you sip chai together.

Index

Find Mira and her brand Chai by Mira online:

www.miramanek.com @miramanek

www.chaibymira.com @chaibymira